Twelve Steps Back to GOD Through Jesus Christ

A Biblically - Based Recovery Program
for
Those Who Are Addicted and Are Substance Abusers

Pastor: Dr. William J. King
of
Living Word Bible Fellowship

Submitted by: Richard S. Lee
Living Word Biblical Counseling Center
48 Cooper Street
Woodbury, New Jersey
08096

AuthorHouse™
1663 Liberty Drive
Bloomington, IN 47403
www.authorhouse.com
Phone: 1-800-839-8640

First published by AuthorHouse 3/4/2010

ISBN: 978-1-4389-6770-7

Printed in the United States of America
Bloomington, Indiana

This book is printed on acid-free paper.

For information contact:

Living Alternative / Biblical Counseling
And Training Center
48 Cooper Street, Woodbury, New Jersey
08096

DEDICATION

Ezra 6:16-18

Than the people of Israel – the Priests, the Levites, and all the others who had returned from exile, joyfully dedicated the Temple. For the dedication they offered a hundred bull 200 sheep, and 400 lambs as sacrifices and twelve goats as offerings for Sin, one for each tribe of Israel. They also organized the Priests and the Levites for the temple services in Jerusalem according to the instructions contained in the book of Moses.

In the early years of my life the late twenties and early thirties, I was involved in the Woodbury Jaycees Project Service to Overcome Drug Abuse among Teenagers. (SODAT)

In the late seventies I was having some problems. My wife and I found Biblical Counseling at Christian Stronghold Baptist Church in Philadelphia. We received the counseling and enrolled in the course for training. I have been involved in Biblical Counseling instruction since the early eighties.

I want to thank my spouse, Loretta, for working with me, giving me the support and the love I needed. I am thanking My Lord and Savior Jesus Christ for the vision and the direction for Biblical Counseling.

TABLE OF CONTENTS

- Personal Data Inventory
- Waiver / Release Commitment
- HIPAA Privacy Notice
- Weekly Counseling Record (1-4)
- Disclosure
- Assignment / Problem Solving
- Survey / Counselor Form
- Release Form / Clients
- Weekly Roundtable Review
- Weekly Case summary
- Counselor Evaluation
- Questionnaire

- Project – Turn-Around

- Promises of Recovery
- Substance Abuser

PROJECTS ACTIVITIES: 94

- **Transportation**
- **Employment Concept**
- **Post-Traumatic Stress Debriefing**

Introduction

The project, Twelve Steps Back To God Through Jesus Christ, is designed to assist its participants in overcoming their drug addiction over a well structured fourteen week period that encompasses four basic areas listed as follows:

- Biblical Counseling
- Biblical Instruction
- Group Sessions
- Career and Educational Counseling

Participants in the project will include two groups. (1) Those to be identified as Clients, as a result of their status as either former inmates or persons conditionally released from the court system. (2) Those students who normally enroll at the Counseling Center to obtain certification as counselors following their successful completion of the four required courses in the program.

The group identified as Clients will be solicited from residential center or treatment center and taken in as a response to court recommendation or referrals from other sources. The group identified as students will be those sponsored by local churches or those paying their own tuition.

To identify the specifics regarding the participant's anticipated changes in their behavior or their performance, the objectives are listed below:

- The program will provide services to 20 to 25 Clients, both male and female per week. Of the total number of Clients receiving services, at least 75% will attend for the entire fourteen week period.
- The program / project will expose (10) students enrolled in the Counseling courses to the fourteen week. Project of the students participating 90% will attend all meeting to learn the progression of steps leading to overcoming addiction.
- The Clients, at least 75%, will become proficient in writing resumes for employment and will develop the skills needing for handling a job interview.

1

- At least 75% of the Clients participating in the program will demonstrate their awareness of G E D programs and other agencies for completing their elementary and secondary education apart from formal traditional schools following their completion of the fourteen week program.
- At least 75% of the Clients participating in the program will demonstrate that they have been assisted in overcoming their drug addiction by:

  1. Submitting to urine analysis testing on a monthly basis.
  2. Signing a pledge to remain drug free
  3. Joining an organized church.

- At least 75% of the Clients in the program will address their medical problems caused by addiction by seeking services following their fourteen week program.
- All students and at least 75% of the Clients will be able to identify addictive behaviors after completing six of the steps in the Twelve Step program.
- After completion of steps seven to twelve, all students and 75% of the Clients will express that they were able to:

  1. Discover new patterns of thinking
  2. Learn the role of restitution and atonement.
  3. Acknowledge the importance of spiritual development.
  4. Examine the importance of reconciliation and restoration with respect to the Lord and to others in their relationships.

ACKNOWLEDGEMENTS

This reference is a result of the combined efforts of many persons who made either direct or indirect contributions to me. I am grateful for the input, encouragement, and above all prayers of a host of friends that include pastors, students, instructors, and family members.

The list of persons and organizations acknowledged include a range of sources that began with my initial venture into counseling and has continued to the present as I seek to deliver counseling services throughout the South Jersey area.

Thanks to Dr. Willie Richardson, Pastor of Christian Stronghold in Philadelphia and Director of the Christian Research and Development Center in Upper Darby, Pa. 19082 for starting me on the counseling path over twenty-five years ago. Supporting these efforts have been others pastors, Rev. W. D. Willis of First Baptist Church of Jericho, Rev. William King of the Living word Bible Fellowship, and Dr. Frank Matthew's of Media Pa.

The Counseling Center operated by the Living Word Bible Fellowship has provided an array of fruitful resources through its capable inspiring students.

I wish to cite special assistance given by Rita Freeney, Gerald Farmer, and Gregory Hoods through their work at the Counseling Center. In addition, experiences and information attained from the National Biblical Counseling Association and Narcotics Anonymous have been invaluable.

Special thanks to my sister, Dr. Mabel C. Lee, for her time given to proofread and comment on earlier versions of this work.

And finally, I want to say thanks to my wife, Loretta, for her constant patience and encouragement to see this project completed.

The list of names and their position in the process has been a help in the development of this concepts in addressing the Twelve Steps Back to God Through Jesus Christ.

Dr. William J. King	Pastor
Dr. Mable C. Lee	Const. / Reader
Dr. Willie Richardson	Pastor / Christian Stronghold
De' An Woodford	B.C. 111 Instructor
Gerald Framer	Biblical Counselor Student
Michael Spencer	Biblical Counselor Student
Joyce McCoy	Biblical Counselor Student
Ronald W. Whitaker 11	Biblical Counselor Student
Theodosia Hart-Trent	Biblical Counselor Student
Roberto Negron	High School Student
Joanne Graham	Biblical Counselor Student
Aimee	Unknown

STATEMENT OF NEED

Drug abuse truly a national problem, has surfaced as a significant problem in the South Jersey and Philadelphia Area. This fact has been clearly demonstrated through the work of the Living Word Biblical Counseling Center located in Woodbury, New Jersey. The center, in operation for twelve years, has provided services for drug addicts either directly or indirectly via its students enrolled in their courses or via its clients referred from a variety of sources.

The center is now prepared to expand its scope of services by instituting the program Twelve Steps Back to God Through Jesus Christ, a recovery program similar to Narcotics Anonymous in its design and delivery of services.

The goal of the program is to identify those clients who are substance abusers and have an addiction problem. The targeted clients will be those who have been recommended from courts or referred from other sources.

The program will provide the individual with a qualified therapist, instructor of Biblical violations, group leader, and individual Career Counseling. The program will need twelve to sixteen weeks for positive results. Clients will be in therapy for two or more sessions a week.

Gloucester Country would be the targeted area to service clients. The program will be able to handle twenty to twenty-five males and females a week, for those who are in the following groups:

- Released from the county jail and between the ages of thirty - five and fifty - five years old.
- Unemployed and physically challenged because of addiction and substance abuse.

PROGRAM DESCRIPTION

This program is designed to help clients to master the <u>Twelve Steps Back to God Through Jesus Christ Program.</u> The clients will be introduced to the biblical principles and precepts which are the propelling force behind the Twelve Steps Back to God Through Jesus Christ Program. The client will learn how to effectively counsel those who are addicted and are substance abusers by using the Twelve Steps Back to God Through Jesus Christ program. The intense review and study of the Twelve Steps Back to God Through Jesus Christ will be based on the same principles as those of Narcotics Anonymous with respect to the way participants progress through the various steps. This program will be set - up in four phases to cover the following areas:

- Biblical Counseling
- Biblical Instruction
- Group Sessions
- Career and Educational Counseling

GOALS:

The goal of the program is to identify clients who are substance abusers and who have an addiction problems, and to assist them in overcoming their problem through the Twelve Steps Back to God Through Jesus Christ Program.

The goal of the program is to have clients involved in a fourteen plus week recovery program. The client will be trained in how to identify addictive behaviors in steps one through six. Clients will also have one - on - one counseling. There will be a group session meeting once a week and biblical instruction class. Healing should take place after each step, and each step will be supported by scriptures from the Bible

Clients will be train in Maintenance Repair, Auto Repair, Ground Care, and to revisit skills they have lost.

GOALS:

Training program in step seven through twelve will show the Client that they can change their behavior of substance abuse. The clients should see and feel physical, mental and social changes in his/her life. They will learn how to handle problems they will encounter through our Lord and Savior, Jesus Christ.

PROGRAM OUTLINE: **(Part One)**

- The origins of addiction
- Discover God's plan for deliverance.
- How to examine recovery profile.
- Understand the role of submission in recovery.
- Self-examination time - uncover your own addictions.
- Understand the power of the role origin of the Twelve Steps Back to God Through Jesus Christ.
- How to effectively prepare for each step.
- practice counseling using the first six steps.
- Completion of Journal entry.

The purposes of step one through six are to:

- Understand your position in your addiction.
- Understand God's power to deliver you from addiction.
- Understand the necessity of giving up the throne of your life.
- Understand your responsibility to others.
- Discover the pattern of sin in your life.
- Acknowledge that obedience to God comes through humility.

GOALS:

Training program in seventh step through twelve will show the Client that they can change their behavior of Substance abuse. The client will see and feel physical, mental and social changes in their lives. They will learn how to handle problems they will encounter through our Lord and Savior, Jesus Christ.

PROGRAM OUTLINE: **(Part Two: Activities)**

- Learn the role of repentance in recovery.
- Learn the role of humility in recovery.
- Understand the discipline of making amends.
- Understand how the old nature and the new nature operate.
- Articulate a new way of thinking.
- Practice counseling using steps seven through twelve.
- Maintain a Journal.

Steps One to Six

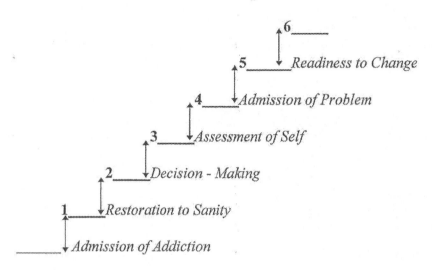

6
5 ↕ *Readiness to Change*
4 ↕ *Admission of Problem*
3 ↕ *Assessment of Self*
2 ↕ *Decision - Making*
1 ↕ *Restoration to Sanity*
↕ *Admission of Addiction*

Program Components:	Time allocated to the Component
• Biblical Therapy	* 12 to 14 weeks
• Biblical Group session	* 4 to 14 weeks
• Biblical Instruction	* 4 to 14 weeks
• Biblical Career / Employment Counseling	* 4 to 14 weeks

The purposes of steps seven through twelve are to:

- Discover new patterns of thinking.
- Learn the role of restitution.
- Understand your responsibility to carry the message to others.
- Acknowledge the importance of spiritual development and growth in the Lord.
- Examine the importance of reconciliation and restoration in relationship.
- Practice the principles of what you have learned.

Program Outline - Part (1)

Steps one through six:

- The origin of addictions and the **Dysfunctional Roots.**

- How to examine **Recovery Profiles** in the Bible.

- Discover God's plan for **Deliverance.**

- Understand the role of **Submission** in recovery.

- Understand the power of the role **Conversion** in recovery.

- **Self - Examination** time to uncover your own addictions.

- Learn the **Christian Foundation** for origin of the Twelve - Step Program.

- How to **Effectively** prepare for each steps.

- Practice **Counseling** using the first six steps.

- **Workbook** completion and **Journal** entry.

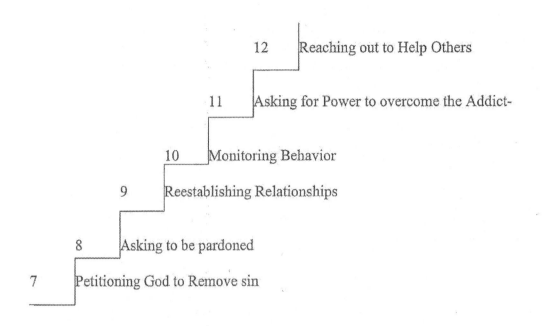

12   Reaching out to Help Others

11   Asking for Power to overcome the Addict-

10   Monitoring Behavior

9   Reestablishing Relationships

8   Asking to be pardoned

7   Petitioning God to Remove sin

STEPS

Notes:

*	Biblical Therapy	12 to 14 weeks
*	Biblical Instruction	4 to 12 weeks
*	Biblical Group Sessions	4 to 12 weeks
*	Biblical Career / Employment Counseling	8 to 12 weeks

Course Outline – Part 2
Spring Semester

Steps seven through twelve:

- Learn the role of **<u>Repentance</u>** in recovery.

- Learn the role of **<u>Humility</u>** in recovery.

- Understand how the **<u>Old Nature</u>** and **<u>New Nature</u>** operate.

- Articulate a new way of **<u>Thinking.</u>**

- Practice **<u>Counseling</u>** using steps seven through twelve.

- Complete **<u>Workbook</u>** and **<u>Joural.</u>**

MAJOR COMPONENTS of the PROGRAM and TIMELINES

Four Phase Process

Weeks:

1. 2. .3   4.   5.   6.   7.   8.   9.   10.   11.   12.

Biblical Counseling:
///

Biblical Instruction:
///

Biblical Sessions:
///

 Career and Educational Counseling:
///

TIMELINES:

The Twelve Steps Back to God Through Jesus Christ Program will
operate in four phases:

- Biblical Therapy............................10th to 12th
  week
- Biblical Instruction.........................4th to 12th
  week
- Biblical Group Sessions....................4th to 12th
  week
- Biblical Career / Educational ....4th to 12th
  Counseling

The Clients will complete the program in twelve plus weeks. They will be
involved in individual therapy for the full twelve weeks. The client will
also be placed in Biblical instructional classes for a period of six weeks.
The client will also be placed in a biblically based group setting. Training
for the client will be set-up to inform them of career and educational
opportunities.

GUIDELINES for MOVING FROM ONE STEP to the NEXT STEP

Twelve Steps Back To God Through Jesus Christ

Steps	Evidence of Steps achieved
1. Admission of Addiction	Admitting that you are powerless over the addiction and unable to manage your life
2. Restoration to Sanity	Believing that, power greater than oneself can restore one's sanity
3. Decision - Making	Deciding to turn your will and life over to God and His care
4. Assessment of Self	Searching and conducting a moral inventory of oneself
5. Admission of the problem to self and to another person	Admitting the exact nature of the Problem to self and another person
6. Readiness to change	Asking God to remove all defective behaviors that mold character
7. Submission to God via petitioning	Asking God to remove shortcomings
8. Request for pardoning	Making amends to all harmed
9. Reestablishment of relationships	Making direct amends to all offended whenever possible
10. Decision to monitor behavior	Continuing to monitor personal behavior to identify straying and the need to revert to the correct way

| 11. Use of power to overcome | Praying and meditating on God to strengthen your relationship with Him |
| 12. Outreach Ministry | Reaching out to help others with addictive problems and utilizing principles in other situations whenever applicable |

RESULTS:

The clients will be able to understand the Twelve Steps from a Biblical perspective.

The clients will be able to clearly recognize the spiritual discipline in experiencing deliverance from their problem.

The clients will be able to effectively understand the role of the following factors play in the recovery process:

- Submission,
- Conversion,
- Confession,
- Repentance,
- Amendments,
- Maintenance, and
- PRAYER in the recovery process.

THE PURPOSE OF EACH STEP IN OVERCOMING
THE ADDICTION

Steps	Purpose
STEP ONE	Understand your position in addiction.
STEP TWO	Understand God's power to deliver you from addiction.
STEP THREE	Understand the necessity of giving up the throne of your life.
STEP FOUR	Understand your responsibility to others.
STEP FIVE	Discover new patterns of sin in your life.
STEP SIX	Acknowledge that obedience to God comes through humility.
STEP SEVEN	Discover new patterns of thinking.
STEP EIGHT	Learn the role of restitution and atonement.
STEP NINE	Understand your responsibility to carry the message to others.
STEP TEN	Acknowledge the importance of spiritual development and growth in the Lord

STEP ELEVEN	Examine the importance of reconciliation and restoration in the Lord.
STEP TWELVE	Examine the importance of reconciliation.

SCHEDULE of ACTIVITIES

Objective to be met:	Activities:	Persons Responsible
1. The program will provide services to 20 to 25 clients both males and female per week.	Referral	Counselor's & Director
2. The program project will expose 10 students enrolled in the BC-4 course to the fourteen week project.	Biblical Counselor Four	Director & Students
3. Dates of Actives, Sept. to May the end of the spring semester.	Director, part Students course Program.	Director & Students
4. Twelve Step program leading to overcoming addition and drugs abuse.	Director & Students	Students
5, Operation of small Biblical group session to identify how clients will handle sin when confronted.	Director	Clients, Counselor
6. Resource counselor to provide Clients with information on careers and education opportunities	Every week	Counselor
7. Maintaining a daily journal for recording experiences to identify end of the of therapy	1st session until	Counselor
8. Preparation for writing resumes	Week (9) of the (14)	Client
9. Role playing for job interviews	Week (9)	Client

10. Recruitment personnel for GED programs providing programs for completion of primary education.	Week (9) 4 Times	Client Director
11. Resource speakers such as medical officers knowledgeable of illnesses emanating from drug abuse.	2 Times	Director

TURN-A-ROUND MINISTRY

What need is the organization seeking to meet?

The goal of the organization is to identify three groups of people who are substance abuses, the inmates who are eligible for release within a two to three month period, their children under the Mentoring program and assist them in overcoming their problem through the "Twelve Steps Back to God Through Jesus Christ" program and Alternative school program. The Gloucester County and surrounding County will see a change in their community.

Adopt-A-School program will need equipment and supplies for all programs, transportation, staff, and space.

Is the problem to be addressed clearly defined?

The State of New Jersey thru Gloucester County One Stop and the County Department of correction thru the chosen Freeholders is sponsoring job fair for those inmates who will be released in two to three months. The Courier Post and The Philadelphia Inquirer, the South Jersey section talk about the Heroin used in the local neighborhoods in Gloucester County and surrounding areas. The affect of drugs used has hurt individual families and entire neighborhoods. Yes! The problem is clearly defined.

What is the proposed program?

The proposed program is to address the problem that people are having base on their drug, alcohol and tobacco used. The Christian Counseling Center in expanding its services by implementing the Twelve Step and drug testing with individual counsel and groups session. We will partner with the public school system for their alternative program and students who can not adjust to public school setting. The recovery program is similar in nature to Narcotics Anonymous.

What is the target population for the project, its size and geographical boundaries?

We have identifying Lakeland in Camden County and Woodbury in Gloucester County the Blackwood site is being used for The Turn -A-Round Program .and the Woodbury Center for Counseling and Careers Technical Education training to be offer.

We are bridging the gap between Residential and the community. The target population will be those who are addicted, problem with school, and those who in transition from prison back into society.

Did the target population have input in the project's development? Overall, how will the target population benefit from the project?

Yes! The clients who are in the program asked for this type of program that they and their family will benefit from the program. The community asked for a program for students who have been asked to leave school before graduation. The local churches recognized that this population needs a difference start in order to change. There are several success stories on file.

How does this project differ similar programs programs or services, how is it unique of different?

- This program will have an Alternative School and a Career Technical Education program for those students who can not adjust to public school setting.
- The program will provide counseling for teens and their family.
- The program is certifying for drug testing for probation and Industry.
- This Program will provide counseling for probation and there plan for drug offenders etc.
- This program will have a Twelve Step Program that includes individual counseling and group therapy for the (18) year olds.
- There will be assignment given on a weekly basic.

What are the specific objectives of the program, and what activities will be carried out to achieve the objectives?

Problems	Drug Addiction	Children's / Family
Counseling	Counseling / Group	Mentoring
8 / 12 weeks	Six Months	12 weeks / Plus
Instruction / Assignment	Drug Testing	Career / Technical
Career / Technical	Employment	Education / Visitations

The goal of the program is to identify those clients who are substance abusers, or addiction problem. Those who have been recommended by other agency and churches.

What is the timetable, and is it realistic?

(Adopt-A-School is set to open   for three years. Students will attend for one year and be evaluated. The school system will identify the students that will qualify for an alternative setting for education. The students will be here until all quantification has been met to satisfy the local board of education.

Twelve Steps Program	Six Months
Biblical Counseling	10/12 weeks
Group Therapy	Six Months / plus
Education / Employment	12/20 plus

The client will be evaluated upon completion of the program in Six months, They will be involved in individual therapy for the full twelve weeks plus. The client will be placed in individual counseling and educational and career and technical program.

GROUP PROCESS

The group process will be used as a means of discussion of issues that the youth are facing today. These are only a few example listed below.

Understanding your emotions.

- Don't seek revenge
- Know yourself
- Learn to recognize the signs of depression
- Keep your hostility in check
- Respect your feeling

A time to learn.

- Learn from the mistakes of other brothers
- Study hard
- Be a listener
- Read, read, read
- Learn even when you're not in school

The topic and many more, for next sixty to ninety days we will give assignment to support your GED program, with reading and writing.

As an out-patient center we can provide services on the second, third, and the fourth Mondays of the month.

The time would be, between (6:00pm – to- 9:00pm). We would provide one counselor, and three mentors and one of them would be a female.

We would also provide form the theater ministry a play or skit for learning proposes.

What about others affected by Biblical counseling but not in Biblical counseling ? The counselee's environment may not change immediately and other people involved may not be seeking GOD. They [others] may not want to change because it will cause them to take a deeper look at themselves and to give up their comfortable [yet sinful] practices. You [counselee] may realize that you or someone you love, has no idea of Godly character - what it is or how to sustain it - and you may have overlooked this in the past, but it is important to you now - as you pass from darkness into His marvelous light. They may even wonder why, (if they are a Christian and saved by the blood of the lamb), is the pull for righteousness and holy living harder on the counselee than themselves to seek the face of GOD; beyond the church pew? Everyone at some point in their life struggles with faith hi GOD.

And there is hope...

To go through this, your counselee must understand their spiritual life, their prayer life and the Word of GOD as keys to their relationship with GOD. The Word of GOD must whisper hi their ear and replace the gossip and backbiting, murmuring and complaining that used to fill the *eye - gate* and *mouth - gate*. The Word of GOD must fill their eyes and replace the once tainted *eye - gate* vision with true sight through His marvelous light. The Word off GOD must fill their soul and change their mind, transforming their actions where they've grown apart from GOD. They have to understand that the change will have to be encountered through fellowship with others in then- family, whether biological or spiritual. The more Christ is being developed hi you, the more [unsaved & unseeking] people will fight to cling to the past, to cling to what was comfortable, secure, and to cling to what they can control.

To the counselee, their prayer life must become not what they do, but what they will do hi the further. They must embrace prayer as Jesus did hi the Garden of Gethsemane as a lifeline to the Father.

Let this mind be in you. which was also in Christ Jesus.
Philippians 2:5

EVEALUATION

The evaluation procedures to be used in assessing the project, Twelve Steps Back To God Through Jesus Christ will result in obtaining both formal and informal data. Questionnaires will be utilized with participants to assess and / or their progress in moving through each step. Formative data will be obtained on a weekly basis in getting informal data. Cumulative data will be obtained at the completion of the program through questionnaires. discussions and group sessions as participants share their feeling in moving from one step to another.

Clients as well as students will be given weekly assignments that are to be completed, graded and discussed. All participants are expected to keep scheduled appointments. Records of completed assignments will be maintained throughout the (14) week project and attendance will be taken at every session.

Clients will be evaluated by several standards.

- Completion of weekly assignments.
- Keeping all appointments.
- Making an immediate change in their life styles.
- Free of all drugs.
- Placement in Education or Employment.
- Their relationship with the Lord.

The Evaluation Chart below explicitly demonstrates how and when each objective will be achieved and assessed:

Evaluation chart

Objective	How it will be achieved	Evidence that the objective has been met

Follow - up questionnaires will be distributed to project participants one month after they have completed the (14) week program. The questionnaire will be designed to investigate four area.

- Plan to complete their elementary / secondary Ed.
- Contact with medical services to address physical problem.
- Plans for employment.
- Evidence of spiritual growth.
- See appendix for copy of questionnaire.

The questionnaire will be sent a second times, at the end of the spring semester to determine the impact of the project.

Courses in the Certification Program are routinely evaluated by its participants at the completion of the semester. (See appendix) for copies of the instrument used to assess the courses and the instructor. The courses in the program include:

Biblical Counseling is the used of the BIBLE, God word to give God example and God solution to your problem.

- Biblical Counseling   1   (Looking at Self)
- Biblical Counseling   2   (Addressing the problem)
- Biblical Counseling   3   (Learning process to help others)
- Biblical Counseling   4   (To help others)

- Plan to complete their elementary / secondary Ed.
- Contact with medical services to address physical problem.
- Plans for employment.
- Evidence of spiritual growth.
- See appendix (2) for copy of questionnaire.

The questionnaire will be sent a second time, at the end of the spring semester to determine the impact of the project.

Courses in the Certification Program are routinely evaluated by its participants at the completion of the semester. (See appendix) (5) for copies of the instrument used to assess the courses and the instructor. The courses in the program include:

Biblical Counseling is the use of the BIBLE, God word to give God example, and God's solution to your problem.

- Biblical Counseling   1   (Looking at Self)
- Biblical Counseling   2   (Addressing the problem)
- Biblical Counseling   3   (Learning process to help others)
- Biblical Counseling   4   (To help others)

Executive Summary:

Drug abuse truly a national problem has surfaced as a significant problem in the South Jersey and Philadelphia area. This fact has been clearly demonstrated through the work of the Living Word Biblical Counseling Center located in Woodbury New Jersey. The center, in operation for ten years, has provided services for drugs' addicts either directly or indirectly via its students enrolled in their courses or via its clients referred from a variety of sources.

The center is now prepared to expand its scope of services by instituting the program Twelve Steps Back to God Throughout Jesus' Christ. A recovery program similar in the natures to Narcotics Anonymous.

The goal of the program is to identify those clients who are substances' abusers and have an addiction problem. The target clients will be those who are incarcerated, in resicertial centers, those from treatment centers, and those who have recommended from courts or referred from other sources.

The program will provide the individual with a qualified therapist instructor of biblical violations, group leader, and individual Career Counseling. The program will need twelve to sixteen weeks for positive results. Clients will be in therapy for two or more session a week.

Gloucester Country would be the target area to service clients. The program will be able to handle twenty to twenty-five males and females a week. .Those who are in the following groups:

    a.   Release from the county jail and between the ages. of thirty - five and fifty-five years old.

    b.   Unemployed, Physically challenged clients because of addiction and substance abuse.

The Counseling Center operated by the Living Word Bible Fellowship has made a significant contribution in South Jersey through the efforts of its certified counselors. With the implementation of the project Twelve Steps Back To God Through Jesus Christ the services will be greater in its scope and in the number utilizing their services.

The counseling program will not only reach those recommended by churches but also those who are in a worse condition because of their problems with the legal system. This special targeted population will also have the potential to reach others after they successfully complete the program. Thus, counseling services will multiply in the South Jersey region.

It is envisioned that once this program has been piloted by the Living Word Biblical Counseling Center, it can be replicated in various churches and regions since the program implemented to the center's certification program will be involved in delivering the program to its clients (Counselee's). Participants in the pilot program will come from varied sources, referrals from the court system, churches, or other agencies. A long - term benefit of this program is the fact that the process is not only confined to overcoming drug addiction but also applying it to other sins such as alcoholism, lying, stealing, etc. Some partitions will be placed in the New Jersey Work Force Program and others in the education sector.

Solution:

To address the drug addiction problem that appears to be the increase and in particular among Black males the center is proposing implementation of program Twelve Steps Back to God Through Jesus Christ. The program is specifically designated to deliver persons from drug addiction through its intense used of four major components.

ORGANIZATIONAL and OPERATION of the CENTER

The Counseling Center operates four days per week, Monday, Tuesdays, Thursdays, and Fridays to provide services for (10) Clients coming for assistance at least once a week for scheduled appointments. The center also provides services for those who walk -- in without scheduled appointments.

Services are provided from 9:00am to 9:00pm daily by the staff that includes the following:

- Three instructors,
- Two administrators,
- Two recorder
- Two Biblical Counselor's

Program Summary:

- Program starting date: September'
- Program ending date: July
- Operation -- Details   Mon. Tues. Thru. Fri.
- Times: From 9:00am to 9:00pm
             (By appointment)

- Number to be served: 12 maximum in each activity
- 12 Clients coming for   10 Biblical Counselors from
  help at least once a   the Senior class will work
  week. We will provide   in the internship program.
  Services for walk ins.

- Plan to complete their elementary / secondary Ed.
- Contact with medical services to address physical problem.
- Plans for employment.
- Evidence of spiritual growth.
- See appendix (2) for copy of questionnaire.

The questionnaire will be sent a second time, at the end of the spring semester to determine the impact of the project.

Courses in the Certification Program are routinely evaluated by its participants at the completion of the semester. (See appendix) (5) for copies of the instrument used to assess the courses and the instructor. The courses in the program include:

Biblical Counseling is the use of the BIBLE, God word to give God example, and God's solution to your problem.

- Biblical Counseling   1   (Looking at Self)
- Biblical Counseling   2   (Addressing the problem)
- Biblical Counseling   3   (Learning process to help others)
- Biblical Counseling   4   (To help others)

Biblical Forms Needed

CASE ATTENDANCE FORM

DATE_____

TIME_____

COUNSELLOR:_____

COUNSELLOR'S ASSISTANT_____

COUNSELEE_____

PRESENT_____ABSENT_____NEXT APPOINTMENT_____

CASE NUMBER_____   SESSION NUMBER_____

    A   ACTIVE CASE

    C   COMPLETED

    T   TERMINATED

    S   SALVATION (RECEIVED CHRIST)

REASON FOR TERMINATION_____

_____

_____

_____

PDI - Personal Data Inventory

IDENTIFICATION DATA

Name				Phone	

Address (include street number, street name, city, state and zip code)

Occupation	Bus. Phone or Cell Phone

Sex	Birth Date	Age

Marital Status:

Single	Going Steady	Married	Separated	Divorced	Widowed	

Education (last year completed)

Other Training: (list type and years)

Referred here by:

Address:

HEALTH INFORMATION

Rate your health:

Very Good	Good	Average	Declining	Other: (explain)

Your approximate weight	lbs.	Recent weight loss	lbs.

Recent weight gain	lbs.	Height

List all important present or pass illnesses, injuries or handicaps:

Date of last medical examination:	Report:
Your Physician:	Address:

Are you presently taking medication?	Yes	No	What type?
Have you used drugs for other than medical purposes?	Yes	No	What?
Have you ever had a severe emotional upset?	Yes	No	Explain
Have you ever been arrested?	Yes	No	Explain
Do you have any legal issues pending	Yes	No	Explain
Are you willing to sign a release of information form so that your counselor may write for social, psychiatric or medical reports?	Yes	No	Explain

RELIGIOUS BACKGROUND

Denominational Preference:			
Are you a member of a church?	Yes	No	
Circle Church attendance per month	1 2 3 4 5 6 7 8 9 10+		
Church Attendance in childhood	Baptized?	Yes	No
Religious background of spouse (if married)			
Do you believe in God?	Yes	No	Uncertain
Do you pray to God?	Never	Occasionally	Often
Have you come to the place in your spiritual life where you can say that you know for certain that if you were to die tonight you would go to heaven?	Yes	No	Uncertain
Are you saved?	Yes	No	Not sure what you mean
Do you have regular family devotions?	Yes	No	
Explain recent changes in your religious life, if any:			

PERSONALITY INFORMATION

Have you ever had any psychotherapy or counseling before?	Yes	No	
If yes, list the counselor or therapist and dates:			
What was the outcome?			

MARRIAGE AND FAMILY INFORMATION

Name of Spouse:			
Address	Phone	Business Phone	
Occupation	Spouse's Age	Education in years	
Is your spouse willing to come to counseling?	Yes	No	Uncertain
Have you ever been separated?	Yes	No	
Separated when? From what dates?			

Has either of you ever filed for divorce?		Yes	No	When?
Date of marriage:	Ages when married?		Husband	Wife
How long did you know your spouse before Marriage?	Years	Months	Other	
Length of dating with spouse	Years	Months	Other	
Length of engagement	Years	Months	Other	
Give brief information about any previous marriages				

Information about children

PM *	Name	Age	Sex	Living? Yes/No	Education In Years	Marital Status

PM* = Child from previous marriage

If you were reared by anyone other than your own parents, briefly explain:

How many older brothers and sisters do you have?	Brothers	Sisters

How many younger brothers and sisters do you have?	Brothers	Sisters

LIVING WORD
BIBLICAL COUNSELING CENTER

(6) BASIC QUESTIONS

Name _____ Date _____

BRIEFLY ANSWER THE FOLLOWING QUESTIONS

1. What is your problem?

2. What have you done about it?

3. What do you want us to do? *(What are your expectations in coming to counseling?)*

4. What brings you here at this time?

5. Is there any other information we should know?

6. Do you belong to a Church?   Yes_____   No_____

   Have you gone to your Pastor for counseling?   Yes_____   No_____

   If no, why not? _____

   If you did, what was the outcome? _____

   Do you think your Pastor would approve of our counseling you? Yes_____ No_____

Biblical Counseling
Disclaimer

We do not claim to be clinical therapists nor lawyers. We do not make any medical or legal claims for any of our work. We are a non-profit ministry that uses counselors that are trained in the word of God. We use biblical principles to assist individuals in solving their problems. We give advice and relevant homework to assist in the decision making process. If a problem arise that is beyond our scope of counsel, we will refer them base on the persons permission to the proper channels.

All information that we collect is for the sole purpose of our counselors/team to review the data to find solutions out of the word of God. We will not disclose any information that is conveyed to us unless it is life threatens, or someone is being abuse. Other information then those mention has to be request by a judge. Our decision is based on the "clergy-communicant privilege", **42 Pa.C.S. 5943** and our church discipline. "Clergy-communicant privilege" is the right of persons who have ministry to prevent testimony in court regarding such communications. Our church discipline is that we will follow Matthew 18 guideline on how to confront an issue. We will not be called or deposed as a witness in any matrimonial disputes. This includes any and all divorce proceedings, custody battles or matters involving legal proceedings between parents of a child or for dissolution of the marital relationship.

By signing below, I acknowledge that counseling/team will assist me in understanding myself and my problems, help me look at alternative solutions and guide me in making my own decisions based on biblical principles. I understand that I am fully responsible for the decisions I make concerning my life or my behavior and recognize that counseling done through this counseling center is pastoral in nature and not under a licensed therapist. I agree not to hold any counselor/team member liable for any actions I may take as result of the counseling I receive.

I have read and fully understand the above information, limits, disclaimers, and consent to counseling as stated. I/We have had an opportunity to ask for additional clarification regarding the conditions herein.

_____   _____
Signature   Printed Name and Date

_____   _____
Counselor's Signature   Printed Name and Date

LIVING WORD BIBLICAL COUNSELING CENTER
WAIVER / RELEASE COMMITMENT

I, the undersigned, certify that I have read the Living Word Biblical Counseling and Training Center brochure and I understand the program as outlined in the brochure. I hereby release Living Word Biblical Counseling Center and Living Word Bible Fellowship Church and it's Pastor, staff, therapist, employees or volunteers from all liability and waive any claim for damage arising from any cause what so ever including not achieving the results expected from the Biblical Counseling Program. I further acknowledge that no one has induced me to be part of the Biblical Counseling Program and that I may terminate the program with notice, at any time, for any reason.

Sign full legal signature: *Print full legal name:*

_____   _____

Date of birth: _____

Witnessed by: _____   *Date:* _____

LIVING WORD BIBLICAL COUNSELING CENTER
48 Cooper Street
Woodbury, New Jersey 08096

COUNSELING DISCLOSURE

All counseling sessions are confidential in nature. However, due to <u>New Jersey</u> Mandatory Reporting Laws, the following topic of information, by law, cannot be treated as confidential and must be disclosed to appropriate authorities:

- *Threats against the physical well being, or life of another person*
- *Suicidal ideation's or threats*
- *Abuse and / or neglect of children*
- *Abuse and / or neglect of elderly individuals*

Your signature on this Disclosure form affirms that you fully understand, acknowledge, and agree to these limitations on confidentiality in participating in counseling.

In a further attempt to safeguard the confidentiality of the counseling process, your signature to this statement confirms that you voluntarily agree not to subpoena information or materials disclosed or generated from counseling sessions, and will not seek to Subpoena or in any way compel testimony of the counselor in any litigation involving a spouse or individual related to the counseling.

It is further acknowledged, by the execution of this Disclosure, that you understand that all counseling offered is pastoral in nature and is not intended to replace counseling offered by mental health professionals.

Dated:_____

Signature:_____

Print Name _____

Sworn and Subscribed to before me this

day of   2005

Notary Public State of New Jersey _____

STATEMENT OF INFORMED CONCENT
Living Word Biblical Counseling Center
48 Cooper Street
Woodbury, New Jersey
08096
(856) 384-8488

Client Name:_____ Date:_____

Address:_____

Telephone #:_____ Date of Birth:_____

Work 3:_____ Cell #:_____

Please accept this authorization as my request for treatment. Service options have been described to me. The services I may M.A. is not available on an "call basis" and that she has instructed me to call emergency services or 911 should an emergency situation arise.

I understand that is not liable for any of my actions outside of the counseling setting.

I understand that all of my sessions will be confidential. I realize that my therapist is obligated under the law to report situations involving the following.

- **Danger to self,** Includes forms of self-injury, inability to care for self, suicidal intent, or noncompliance with essential medical treatment.
- **Danger to others,** Includes homicidal or genocidal ideation
- **Child / elder abuse,** Includes abuse of children or the elderly

Client Signature:_____ Date:_____

Parent/Guardian Signature:_____ Date:_____

I understand that the authorization above is written as if applicable to me, but I ask you to accept it as applicable to my child / ward. Of course, all explanations referred to above been, and when appropriate, will be in the future, given to me.

Parent / Guardian Signature:_____ Date:_____

_____
Counselor's Name

Name _____   Date _____

Session Number: _____

Drift of the Session	New Homework Thoughts

AGENDA ONE/ Session One

Greeting

Basic Questionnaire

Fill out PDI

Explain Program
Ask about continuing

Review PDI for Salvation

Open with Prayer

Review Basic Questions

Share Scripture:
    Homework
    Change
    Hope

Assignment

Appointment

Donation

Close in Prayer

Session Two / Four

Objective:

- Share scriptures on Biblical Violation
- Identify Biblical Violation
- Collect new data and give Hope

Assessment:

To specify the Client's behavioral, which if changed, lead to adaptive function.

Process:

- Greeting
- Open with prayer
- Review the assignment given last week
- Share scripture on Biblical Violation from last weeks notes. *(name the Violation)* you are only planting a seed.
- Collect data: The therapist should have devolve a list of questions from last weeks session. *(pleases noted the responses to each question asked)*
- Share scriptures on Hope / Change
- Assignment / Appointment
- Close in prayer / donation

WEEKLY COUNSELING RECORD

_____

Counselor's Name

Name_____   Date_____

Session Number:_____

Evaluation of last week assignment: New Homework Thoughts

Drift of the session:

AGENDA TWO/ Sessions 2-4

Greeting

Open with Prayer

Review Homework Assignment
   Attend Sunday Service
   Bible Study
   Prayer Meeting
   Sunday School

Share a scripture on the biblical violation presented

Gather Data through the questions you've prepared

Give them scriptural hope from the bible

Scripture on change

Give homework assignments

Assignment

Appointment

Donation

Close in Prayer

Session Five / End

Objectives:

- Addressed one of the Biblical Violation that has been identified in early session. One each week,
- Give solution and Hope. *(for each biblical violation)*

Intervention:

To modify or transform the Client's pattern into a more adaptive pattern.

Share all Biblical Violation and the Root problem. *(note)* By the 4th session, the Therapist will have collected data from 50 to 60 responses. The therapist will addressed one Violation each session.

Teaching Process:

- Last week assignment should be the Biblical Violation that will be addressed in the next session.
- Share what the world says about the Biblical Violation.
- Share from the Bible scriptures on what God says about the Sin.
- Give Biblical solutions from God word to solve the problem. *(note: Be specific with the solution, we must give step by step to solve the problem)* This process should cover a three week span.

Process:

- Greeting
- Open with prayer *(note: you may want to ask the client to open in prayer)*
- Review Assignment: *(have them be vary specific on what they did and how they did it)*
- The Biblical Violation you will addressed will have their assignment for last session.
- Assignment *(Give assignment on this session Biblical Violation and next session Biblical Violation that you will addressed) You will have cover tree session on one Biblical Violation.*

_____

Counselor's Name

Name_____ Date_____

Session Number:_____

Drift of the Session	New Homework Thoughts
Evaluation of last week assignment:	
Drift of the session:	**AGENDA THREE/Sessions 5- final session**
	Greeting
	Share what the root cause of the sin is
	Share what the world says about that sin
	Give them biblical people in the bible that went through that issue
	Hold a mirror up to them and show them what is going on
	Share a biblical solution for what to do
	Assignment
	Appointment
	Donation
	Close in Prayer

Last Session:

Objective:

- Review all Biblical violation and identify the Root Problem.
- Review solution and Hope for change in you through the scriptures.

Maintained / Termination:

- To review each Biblical Violation and what God says about it.
- To share that the world is not going to change you, but God can change you.
- To encourage what has been done in the last sessions on Biblical Violation.

Note: The Clients has completed the therapy session. The Therapist will continues to pray for the Clients and encourage them to contuse there change they have made. The Therapist will show how the Biblical Violation, support the Root problem and the change they have made.

LIVING WORD BIBLICAL COUNSELING CENTER
COUNSELING SURVEY

Client's Name:_____   Date session begins:_____

Counselor:_____   Date session terminated:_____

Number of sessions:_____

Specific problems	Date	Resolved	Resolution
1.			
2.			
3.			
4.			
5.			
6.			
7.			
8.			
9.			
10.			

HIPAA PRIVACY NOTICE

FOR OUR COUNSELING CLIENTS

**Living Word Biblical Counseling Center
(effective April 14, 2003)**

Authorization to Release Information (please print)

This form is used for you or your personal representative to authorize the Service Provider to release your protected health information to another person or organization at your request.

"Protected health information", means individually identifiable heath information. It is information about you, including your name, address and medical information and may relate to your past, present or future physical or mental health condition. The organization maintains information that may include benefits or payment information.

Client Information: (individual whose information will be released)

Print your complete Name, Address, Date of Birth and Telephone Number. Provide your group name and number if available. A Social security number is not required.

Service Provider: (organization that will release your information)

The service provider is the organization that maintains information about you. Print the name of the service provider on the line provided.

Recipient: (person or organization that will receive your information)

The recipient is a person or organization that you choose to receive your protected health information from the Organization. You must provide all of the contact information in order for the information to be released.
* Identify the person, family member or organization to receive your information.
* Provide the contact information about the person, family member or organization.

Description of the Information to be Released: (what type of information will be released)

You must indicate or describe the information to be released. Check one box that best describes your request. There are three choices. The first choice is Psychotherapy Notes. The second choice is All information. The third choice is Specific Information that you must describe on the line provided.

> *If this authorization is to release psychotherapy notes, the organization cannot release any other information unless you complete another Authorization for Release Information Form.*

Psychotherapy Notes are notes recorded by a mental health professional documenting or analyzing the contents of a conversation during a private counseling session or a group, joint, or family counseling session. These notes are separated from the rest of the individual's medical record. Psychotherapy notes cannot be combined with an authorization to release any other type of information.

All Information. If you check this box the Service Provider may release all information including information related to the provision of a payment for any services. If someone is directly involved in coordinating your health care or benefits, you may want them to have access to all of your information.

Specific Information. By checking this box you indicate that you want only specific information to be released. Describe the specific information on the line provided.

Purpose of Release. You must provide a brief description of the reason you want this information released. The statement, " At my request" is sufficient.

IMPORTANT: State law requires that you give specific permission to release certain health information. Your initials are required on each line in order for the organization to release information for HIV/AIDS, Substance/Alcohol Abuse, Genetic Information, Financial, Court Mandated or Mental/Behavior Health Information.

Expiration: (when this authorization will end)

Print wither an expiration date OR event, but not both. If an expiration event is used, the event must relate to the purpose of the release of information being authorized.

Approval: (You OR your personal representative must sign and date this form in order for it to be complete.)

Client Signature.	Personal Representative Information.
If you are the individual whose information will be released, you must sign and date in this section.	If you are the personal representative, the client's signature is not required. However, you must provide the requested information, signature and date. A copy of the legal authority, such as Power of Attorney or other court initiated document, must be on file with the organization.

PLEASE KEEP A COPY OF THIS FORM AND THE INSTRUCTIONS FOR YOUR RECORDS

2003

49.

RELEASE FORM

(Completed by Therapist)

Therapist Evaluation:

Root Problem: _____

_____

Client's Subjective Evaluation: _____

_____

_____

Therapist's Objective Evaluation: _____

_____

_____

Future Plans: _____

_____

_____

General Comments: _____

_____

LIVING WORD CHRISTIAN COUNSELING CENTER

RELEASE FORM
(Completed by Client)

NAME_____ DATE_____

1. **What was your major problem?**

2. **How did the situation become your problem?**

3. **How was the problem (s) solved?** *(Or)* **How was I enabled to live with the problem (s)?**

4. **How will you prevent having the problem again?**

RELEASE FORM
(Completed by Therapist)

Therapist Evaluation:

Root Problem (s)

Client's Subjective Evaluation:

Therapist's Objective Evaluation:

Future Plans:

General Comments:

Living Word Bible Fellowship

Questionnaire

{Directions: To be administered when clients begin the program. Please answer each question in detail}.

1. Has <u>Jesus</u> been in your life most of the time? Give evidence to support your answer.

   _____

   _____

   _____

2. When you thought about getting <u>High</u>, how did you handle the thought?

   _____

   _____

3. List the ministry you have been working in what change you have made, and tell if it was noticed?

   _____

   _____

   _____

4. How has your family been treating you ?

   _____

   _____

5. Please explain responsibilities on your job?

   _____

   _____

Questionnaire

{ Note: This will be administered the second time after your fifth session}.

1. What has the Lord done for you? Please explain with an example.

    _____

    _____

    _____

2. Please explain your employment situation and your financial status?

    _____

    _____

3. What do the people who live in your house say about you?

    _____

    _____

4. Would you be willing to come for an interview?

    _____

5. Please explain your involvement in your church or the church you attend ?

    _____

    _____

LIVING WORD BIBLICAL COUNSELING CENTER
WEEKLY ROUNDTABLE REVIEW

Lead Therapist _____   <u>Session Date:</u> _____

Asst. Therapist: _____   <u>Session Number:</u> _____

Counselee: _____

Agenda	Homework Assignment	Completed
1.	1.	
2.	2.	
3.	3.	
4.	4.	
5.	5.	
6.		
7.		
8.		
9.		

1. **Briefly describe the case,** including the key items of information from the PDI and *"Drift of the Session"*. Please remember: exclude any details that might enable the counselee (s) to be identified by anyone reading this case summary (i.e. name, location of church, name of people, proper names, etc.)

2. **Drift of the session:** *including "Halo Data"*

3. List Biblical Violation (s) Found

    1.

    2.

    3.

    4.

    5.

    6.

4. Indicate Biblical Violation (s) being addressed this session, *including 4 P's and put – ons " put – offs" with supporting scriptures*

Presentation (feeling) problem?_____

_____

Performance (doing) problem _____

_____

Preconditioning (root problem? _____

_____

Pattern of Thinking (mindset) problem? _____

_____

    "Put Offs"   "Put Ons"

    _____   _____

    _____   _____

    _____   _____

4. **Indicate biblical violation(s) being addressed this session,** *including 4 P's and "put-ons" & "put-offs" with* *supporting scriptures*

Presentation (feeling) problem?

_____

Performance (doing) problem?

_____

Preconditioning (root) problem?

_____

Pattern of Thinking (mindset) problem?

_____

| *"PUT OFFS"* | *"PUT ONS"* |

_____

5. **List remaining session(s) and violation(s) to be addressed**

LIVING WORD BIBLICAL
COUNSELING and TRAINING CENTER
48 COOPER STREET
WOODBURY, NEW JERSEY 08096

Director: Pastor William King   **Telephone: (856) 384-8488**
Supervisor: Richard S. Lee

To: Gloucester, Camden County Courts
From: Living Word Counseling Center
Re: Courts Referral

Greetings from the Living Word Biblical Counseling.
This is a report to indicate client's progress with Counseling.

Date started _____

Time of session _____

Clients name _____

Counselor name _____

Co-Counselor name _____

Today's date _____

	No	Yes
a. Has the client kept all of his/her appointments?		
b. Has clients followed all guidelines?		
c. Has the client been Drug and Alcohol free?		
d. Has the client completed all assignments?		
e. Should counseling continue for another four weeks?		
f. The counseling sessions should be terminated?		
g. Client has completed all requirements for counseling?		

This report will be completed every week.

BIBLICAL COUNSELOR EVALUATION FORM

EVALUATOR_____

EVALUATEE_____

	EXCELLENT	GOOD	NEED IMP.	POOR
GREETING				
BASIC QUESTION				
PDI				
EXPLAIN PROGRAM				
OPEN PRAYER				
REVIEW BASIC QUESTION				
SIN INDENTIFICATION				
PLAN OF SALVATION				
TAKEING NOTES				
BUILDING HOPE				
SCRIPTURE ON CHANGE				
UESD OF THE BIBLE				
BIBLICAL VIOLATIONS				
GATHER DATA				
LOVE AND COMPASSION FOR COUNSELEE				
10 OR MORE QUESTION				
CONFRONTATION				
SCRIPTURE KNOWLEDGE				
PREPARATION AND RESEARCH				
HOMEWORK ASSIGNMENTS				
REVIEW				

LIVING WORD BIBLICAL COUNSELING CENTER
SERVEY RELEASE FORM

Counselor Name:_____   Date:_____

Counselee Name:_____

1.   What was your major problem when you came for Biblical Counseling?

_____

_____

2.   What was your problem after the fifth session?

_____

_____

3.   How did the problem become your problem?

_____

_____

4.   How was the problems solved? *(Please explain)*

_____

_____

5.   How will you handle problems that will come – up in the further? *(Please explain)*

_____

_____

| BC - III Handout | **CASE SUMMARY** |

Format for Case Summary Reports

☐ Weekly

☐ Final

1.

Submitted By:			Date of Report:	
		Lead Counselor	Case Number:	
		Assistant Counselor	Number of Sessions:	
		Assistant Counselor	Average Length of Sessions:	

2.

Age _____

Marital and Family Status _____

State of Health _____

Medical Care and Medication _____

Religious Background _____

3.

Briefly describe the case, including the key items of information from the PDI and *"Drift of the Session"*. *Please Remember*: exclude any details that might enable the counselee (s) to be identified by anyone reading this case summary (i.e. name and location of the church, actual names of people, proper names, etc).

4.

What is the present situation in regard to this case?

5.

Presentation (feeling) problem?

Performance (doing) problem?

Preconditioning (root) problem?

6.

Describe the kind of relationship the counselee has with each person involved in this problem.

7.

What is the degree of the counselee's spiritual commitment? (How is it demonstrated?)

8.

Describe the halo data as the session progressed.

9.
How is/was the counselee utilizing spiritual resources before counseling? Now? (Include as a minimum, description of devotional life, church life, and help from family members.)

10.

Highlight major points (agenda items) and Scriptures stressed	Describe associated responses and in the counselee

11.

List agenda items yet to be covered in order of priority:

12.
List *Key Homework* assigned:

13.
What structuring is/was necessary in the counselee? To what degree are put-ons/put-offs built into his/her way of life?

14.
Number of remaining sessions/Reason for concluding the case

15.
What follow-up or referral action is taking/took place?

Living Alternative of South Jersey and Vicinity Inc.

Mission:

Project, Turn – Around is a social out reach with the mission to rebuild communities from the inside out with a comphensive faith-based program designed to improve and enrich the lives of urban youth and families.

Goals:

Project Turn-Around provides a hand-up not a hand –out.

Project Turn-Around provides holistic long-term, not short-term solutions by meeting needs in a way that change how people think, which ultimately determines how they live.

Project Turn-around addressed the critical needs of at-risk youth and families with an array of services that include:
- Adopt-a-school program
- Family support services
- Computer technology in education
- Career development
- After-school programs, sports and human needs assistance.

Project Turn-a-Around will provides a myriad of services that sexual abstinence, drug and alcohol used, school drop-out, violence and family support systems.

Youth build Grant Program Components:

We will services youth in South Jersey and Vicinity who face huge dropout rates, massive involvement with legal system, few housing options and excessive unemployment rates.

Project Turn-a-Around objective is to implement an 18 month (Youth Build Program) for 60 youth, aged 14 to 24, to become independent.

The youth will be high school dropouts, grade level repeaters, and low income residents of South Jersey. The program will include test scores, prep on-site training, leadership development, community services social support services, entrepreneurial training, job / apprenticeship placement, and follow on education, placement follow-up.
Project Turn-a-Round will run on open entry program and open exit program with six months as the minim participation period and will enroll additional students beyond the first six months.

Project Turn-a-Round comprehensive, consistent counseling at each stage of program implementation, from out reach to post placement, based on years of working with young adults with few options during outreach, case managers address groups, dropouts, incarcerated and paroled youth. Those not eligible for Project Turn-a-Round are referred to other resources.

THE PROCESS for ADDRESSING BIBLICAL VIOLATION

Twelve Steps Back to God Through Jesus Christ
Promises of Recovery

- We must be saved .

- We are going to know a new freedom and a new happiness.

- We will understand serenity, and we will know peace.

- No matter how far down the scale we have gone, we will see how our experience can benefit others.

- The feeling of uselessness and self-pity will disappear.

- We will lose interest in selfish things and gain interest in our fellows.

- Self – seeking will slip away.

- Our whole attitude and outlook upon life will change.

- Fear of people and economic insecurity will leave us.

- We will intuitively know how to handle situations that use to baffle us.

- We will suddenly realize that GOD is doing for us what we could not do for ourselves.

The Twelve Steps for Those Who Were Addicted
and
Substance Abuser

- We admit we need God's gift of Salvation, that we're powerless over certain areas of our lives, and that our lives are at times sinful and unmanageable.
- We come to believe through the Holy Spirit that a power that came in the person of Jesus Christ and that is greater than ourselves can transform our weaknesses into strengths.
- We make a decision to turn our will and our lives over to the care of Christ as we understand Him more fully.
- We make a searching and fearless moral inventory of ourselves - both our strengths and our weaknesses.
- We admit to Christ, to ourselves, and to another human being the exact nature of our Sins.
- We become entirely ready to have Christ heal all of these defects of character that prevent us from having a more spiritual lifestyle.
- We humbly ask Christ to transform all of our shortcomings.
- We make a list of all people we have harmed and become willing to make amends to them all.
- We make direct amends to such people wherever possible except when to do so would injure them and / or others.
- we continue to take personal inventory, and when we are wrong, promptly admit it and when we are right, thank God.
- We seek through prayer and meditation to improve our conscious contact with Christ as we understand Hi, praying for knowledge of His will for us and the power to carry that out.
- Having experienced a new sense of spirituality as a result of these steps and realizing that this sense is a gift of God's grace, we are willing to share the blessing of His love and forgiveness with others and to practice the principles for spiritual living in all our affairs.

Admission of Addiction
Step One

"We admitted that we were powerless over our addiction, and that our lives had become unmanageable." Rom. 3:10-12

When we accept the fact that we have sinned and we want to change, there is hope. When we come to terms with our addiction, with our recovery, we will not dread the future, but see recovery as a precious gift from GOD and the work connected with it.

- I have made peace with the fact that I'm in Sin (addict). Ps. 51:5
- I have made peace with my GOD that I will stay clean. Ps. 51:7-10
- I have accepted my Sin (addiction) as a confession to GOD and to his willingness to forgive. Ps. 51:14-17

Questions:

Have I truly gained an understanding of this first step?

Answer: YES

Explanation: I have found out that what has been helpful to me is to read and study scriptures and to put my understanding in writing.

- The spirit of the Lord has shown me to move to the next step.
- The spirit has shown me that I was in Sin and needed to repent.
- The experience and knowledge has affected my change for the good.

We've come to a place where we can see the results through the Holy Spirit of our old way of life. You probably will not see immediately how rich with possibilities the life of recovery is. You may have some freedom from active addiction immediately, but you will soon find that the void you have been filling with drugs or other obsessive and compulsive behaviors begs to be filled with something else. The Holy Spirit and the rest of the steps will fill that void.

Restoration to Sanity

Step Two

"We came to believe that a
Power greater than ourselves could
restore us to sanity."

Read and study the scriptures and put in writing your understandings. This will help you to internalize the spiritual principles and concepts connected to the sin you were in.

Spiritual Principles / Concepts:

- The action I can take that will help me along in the process is to continue to read and study the word.
- I will continue to work on overcoming any unrealistic expectation that I may have about being restored to the Lord.
- The understanding of this step is repentance.

There is hope in our spirit. This is not new in recovery; we've just reinforced your knowledge that recovery, growth, and change are inevitable when you make the effort to work the steps. You will see the possibility of relief from the particular brand of insanity in which you most recently have been gripped by Sin (addiction). You probably have already begun to experience some freedom. You have begun to be released from the blind pursuit of your sin (insanity). You have explored your sin (insanity) and have started to trust the Holy Spirit and to relieve yourselves from having to continue on the same path.. You are a secret. You have seen how the Twelve Steps Back to GOD plan has worked for beginning to be freed from your illusions. You no longer have to stuggle to keep your addiction from others, and you have discovered that it is beginning to work for you as well.

Decision - Making

Step Three

"We made a decision to turn our will and our lives over to the care of GOD as we understood Him."

Questions:

- Do I have any reservations about my decision to turn my will and my life over to God's care?
- Do I feel that I am now ready to turn my life over to GOD ?
- How does the confession of my sin in the first step help me in the third step ?
- I know that my Lord and Savior died for my sin and was buried and raised from the dead and lives within me.
- What action do I plan to take to follow through on my decision ?
- How does working the remainder of the steps fit into this plan ?

We have been through this step, and we're profoundly relieved to realize that the world will go along just fine without our intervention. We may feel comforted to know that a loving God is caring for our life, yes, and letting you know in subtle ways that the path we're on is the right one.

Some people pause before making major decisions and ground themselves in their own spirituality. We look to the source of our strength, invite the Holy Spirit to work in my life., and then move forward once we're sure we're on the right track. On that note, we need to take another step along the path of recovery.

Assessing Ourselves

Step Four

"We made a <u>searching</u>
<u>and fearless moral inventory</u>
of ourselves."

You have finished the fourth step. It maybe a letdown; it may be exhilarating; or it may be uncomfortable. However, you will definitely feel good about what you have accomplished. The work you have done in this step will provide the foundation for the work you will do in steps five through nine. Now is the time to contact your career counselor.

(Proverbs   10:1, 13:13, 14:14,15, 15: 11, 31-33, 16:2,3 19:19

                     20:1, 19,20, 21:9, 22:24,25, 23:27,29-35, 25:28

                     26:20-22, 29:1,11,20,22)

(Psalm   66:18, 73:21,22, 90:8)

Admission of Problem
Step Five

"We admitted to GOD, to ourselves, and to another human being the exact nature of our wrong."

One of the benefits of step five is gaining a sense of self-acceptance. We begin to see that we have both assets and defects. We're capable of doing good as well as inflicting harm. However, accepting ourselves as we are today doesn't mean that we can relax and stop striving for improvement.

All of your relationships begin to change as a result of working through this step. We especially need to acknowledge how much our relationships with ourselves, with the Holy Spirit and with other people have changed.

Questions:

- How has your relationship with the Holy Spirit changed as a result of working through this step?
- How has my relationship with my counselor changed as a result of working through this step?
- How has my view of myself changed as a result of working through this step?
- To what extent have I developed love and compassion for myself and other

(Proverbs: 30:32,33, 28:13,14, 27;17, 21:2. 16:118),

(Psalm: 32:3-5, 40:11-13, 51:3,4, 62:8 69:5, 119:66,67)

Readiness to Change
Step Six

"We were entirely ready to have <u>GOD remove all these defects of character.</u>"

You had a glimpse of the past showing what you could have become, perhaps during childhood, or maybe during your active addiction. In the spiritual program, Twelve Step Back To God, we're more concerned with spiritual growth.

We want to get from this step a future vision of ourselves and a sense of hope that we can attain that vision.

Questions that I must ask myself are:

- What do I see myself doing with the qualities I wish to attain?
- What will I do with my career?
- What will I do in my spare time?
- What kind of parent, child, partner, or friend will I be?

This vision will be inspirational and your springboard to leap into step seven is where you will to remove all desire to shoot up.

- Empowered by Christ, the vine, we can and must bear much fruit. (John 15:1-5)
- God will enable you to change and you must . (Phil. 2:12,13)
- God calls you to put off old sinful ways and to put on new and godly ways. (Eph. 4:17-3)

Petitioning GOD to Remove Sin

Step Seven

"We humbly asked Him to remove our shortcomings."

We've asked God of our to remove our shortcoming as we faithfully practice the principles of the Twelve Step Back To God Program to the best of our ability. We may still find ourselves acting out before thinking and struggling with defective traits.

Questions:

- Have there been times when you have been able to refrain from acting on a character defect and instead practiced a spiritual principle instead?
- Did you recognize this as God working in your life?
- Which shortcomings have been removed from your life or diminished in their power over you?

You begin to live a more spiritual life. You will be able to hold up your head with dignity and maintain your integrity no matter what life presents. As you begin to get more comfortable with your spiritual self, your desire to heal your relationships will grow.

Scriptures:

- Put much effort into living a godly life. 11 Peter 3:14
- Use the whole armor of God. Eph. 6:10-17
- Resist the devil. James 4:7
- No longer use your body to sin but to serve God. Rom. 6:10-23
- Cast off all that hinders you. Heb. 12:1

Asking to be Pardoned

Step Eight

"We made a list of all persons we had harmed, and became willing to make amends to them."

You have been clean for a long time; as a result you have many years of experience with making amends every one of you is liable to misjudge a situation when working alone, but we often find that we can see things more clearly when we look at situations from another point of view. You need your counselor's insight, encouragement, vision and hope. When you have stripped away the distracting influences, you have exposed that solid core of serenity, humility and forgiveness.

Biblical Scriptures: (Proverbs 14:1)   (Psalm 133:1-3)

- We must forgive our debtors. (Matt. 6:12)
- Forgiving others is an absolute necessity. (Matt. 6:14,15)
- Jesus says we must forgive often. (Matt. 18:21,22)
- Put away bitterness and anger, forgive as God forgives. (Eph. 4:31,32)
- Jesus commands us to forgive others. (Mark 11:25)
- Love keeps no record of wrongs. (1 Cor. 13:5)
- Love covers a multitude of sins. (1 Peter 4:8)

Reestablishing Relationships

Step Nine

"We made direct amends to
people we have offended wherever possible"

Questions:

- How did it feel to make amends?
- What did I learn about myself after making amends?

Step nine seems to gives us relief from guilt and shame, and it lessens our obsession with ourselves. We increase our ability to appreciate what's going on around us as it is happening. In order to keep this feeling of freedom, you will need to keep applying what you learned in the previous steps.

(Proverbs: 25:11, 16:20-24, 15:1-4, 12:18-20, 3:27)

(Psalm: 51:14-17, 126:5,6)

Monitoring Behavior

Step Ten

**"We continue to take personal
inventory and whenever we stray in the
wrong direction we promptly admit it
and revert to the correct way."**

When you come to full recovery, you realize that you have never been able to have any kind of long-term relationship. The relationship was certainly not one in which you resolved conflicts in a healthy and mutually respectful way.

It becomes more natural for us to admit when we're wrong. We wonder why we ever found it so terrifying.{You felt in so many ways, that an admission of a mistake revealed your deepest secret and your inferiority}. You found out through working the steps that you weren't inferior at all. You realize you had just as much value as anyone else. You realize it no longer seems so crushing to admit that you were wrong.

The freedom that you have been building since the beginning of step one yields an increase in our choices and options. You have total freedom to create any kind of life you want for yourself. You begin to look for meaning and purpose in your life. You ask yourselves if the lifestyle you have chosen helps the still-suffering addict or makes the world a better place in some other way.

Biblical Scriptures:
- The Lord's prayer is our model.
- Pray for daily needs.
- Pray daily for the forgiveness of sins. (Matt. 6:9-13)
- Cast all your anxiety on the Lord. (1 Peter 5:6-7)

Power to Overcome

Step Eleven

**"We sought through prayer
and meditation to improve our
conscious contact with God
as we understood Him,
praying only for knowledge of
His will for us and the power
to carry that out."**

During your regular practice of meditation, you may notice that you are now able to listen more attentively to what others have to say in meetings. You have some experience with quieting your mind and you no longer find yourselves consumed with planning what you will say when it's your turn.

You will no longer feel such an urgency to control things because you will focus on your Lord and Savior, Jesus Christ instead of yourself. Your active addiction no longer seems like such a tragedy and a waste. You see how you can use that experience to serve Jesus Christ. You will be carrying the message to addicts who still suffer.

Biblical Scriptures:

- God cares for the birds and the flowers and certainly He will care for His children. (Matt. 6:25-34)
- God controls all the forces of nature and provides for all His creatures, especially His children. (Ps. 104, Ps. 145, Ps. 147)

Reaching Out to Help Others

Step Twelve

**"Having had a spiritual awakening as a result of
these steps, try to carry this message to addicts,
and try to practice these principles
in all affairs."**

You will continue trying to practice the spiritual principles of the Twelve Steps Back to God, which many call living the program. When we find ourselves powerless over our addiction, we will remember that the steps are always available as our path to recovery.

You should feel good about what you have done. You have in many cases for the first time, followed a process all the way through. One of the rewards of working the Twelve Steps Back to God Program is finding that our self-esteem will grow tremendously.

When you think about where you came from and what your recovery has brought to you, you can only be overwhelmed with gratitude. Your very life will be an expression of your gratitude; it all depends on how you choose to live your life.

The Twelve Steps Back to God WORKS

Pastor William J. King

AGENCY REPORT

by

Stephen Houts

Agency Visited:	Living Word Biblical Counseling Center 48 Cooper Street Woodbury, NJ 08096 (856) 384-8488
Contact Person:	Mr. Richard Lee, Director
Date of Visit:	Thursday, October 9, 2003

Introduction to Counseling
Professor Edward R. Mosley
November 2003

The Living Word Biblical Counseling Center is located in the historic city of Woodbury. The Center is housed in a converted house that has been renovated to include a reception area, offices, meeting rooms, and partitioned conference areas.

During my visit I had the opportunity to sit in on a roundtable type discussion with several counselors at the Center. Due to confidentiality, client names are not used at these weekly discussions. One counselor was discussing a client who was going through a divorce. After several minutes of dialog with the group of counselors, the consensus was that although the client was trying to make progress, the root of this client's anger had not yet been revealed. Until the cause was uncovered, the anger issue could not be fully addressed for positive action.

Following the roundtable discussion, a young man was introduced and given the opportunity to address the group for ten minutes. Although the gentleman has a speech impediment, he has a strong desire to speak to groups, such as in a church setting. The Center is working with this individual to allow him time to gain experience in speaking before groups and improving his verbal message skills. He distributed a handout he had prepared and spoke about individuals with handicaps. He related his own handicap to individuals in the Bible, that of Moses, who at first protested that he was not a great orator, and also to Paul, who had an affliction which is not known. The young man completed his message, with a warm response from his audience.

The counselors then went to their meeting areas and Mr. Richard Lee led me to his office to be interviewed. Mr. Lee was very professional during the interview and had much knowledge about counseling. He was extremely helpful in answering my questions. Mr. Lee explained that he and his wife had founded the Living Word Biblical Counseling Center 25 years ago.

Some of the types of counseling services offered are for marriage problems, drug abuse, and alcohol abuse. In addition, the Center offers career counseling to help individuals learn the necessary skills employers want, prepare resumes, and secure employment. The majority of the clients are African American, but the Center is open to everyone. Clients come to the Center, some recommended from other pastors, phone book, Alcoholics Anonymous, recently released from prison, and word of mouth.

Funding for the Center comes in the form of donations. Local churches may donate funds and supplies. In addition, clients are given a brown envelope for anything they feel they can give, but it is not mandatory. The Center is operated more as an outreach to help the community rather than to make a profit. Counselors are volunteers who may be reimbursed for travel expenses, food and the like. The counselors are dedicated to helping others in their Christian walk, helping them to get back on their feet because they may be struggling at that time.

Staffing for the Center includes the Director, the Director's wife, and several counselors. Mr. Richard Lee oversees the entire Center. Mrs. Loretta Lee performs numerous secretarial duties, including answering the phone, setting up appointments, and scheduling counseling sessions for individuals and groups as necessary. The Center is attached to basically one church, although pastors and elders from other churches participate.

The Living Word Biblical Counseling Center offers courses for training in Biblical counseling through Christian Research & Development (CRD Training Institute) and Living Word Bible Fellowship. Classes range from "Learn How to Use the Bible to Solve Your Problems," a 14 week training course in how to use the Bible to counsel oneself first, then others, to "Biblical Counseling Internship," a 14 week training course where students assist senior counselors and counsel under supervision. Students who successfully complete the four courses are eligible to receive Biblical Counseling Certification.

At the initial interview session, the client is talked to about his/her salvation. The client is then given a questionnaire to complete. This allows the client to state what he/she feels is the problem and gives the counselor a starting point for area(s) to be addressed. In addition, a Personal Data Inventory is completed to provide a rounded background for the counselor. Questions range from "Last year of education" to "Are your presently taking medication?" to "How many older/younger brothers/sisters?" The counselor and client will read from the Bible, not preprinted or copied verses. The counselors at the Center feel it is very important for the client to seek answers in God's Word.

After the initial session, the counselor will work out a schedule with the client. In many cases, clients are given homework assignment(s) to complete in between sessions. These may be attend a weekly Bible study, write out an activity, practice a particular task, etc., depending on the individual case. Once the problem(s) have been identified, Biblical answers are sought. Biblical violations (the problems) are recorded on a case sheet by the counselor, along with other data such as benchmarks set and progress made. Some clients will continue on in group counseling where, Mr. Lee commented, the group puts verbal pressure on individuals to talk out their problems and stay on course.

In conclusion, the Living Word Biblical Counseling Center is a valuable community resource. The counseling services provided are definitely a positive in today's society. The Center provides support for a food bank, job assistance, and housing assistance for individuals in need. The Center had recruited retired school teachers to tutor teenagers when the need had arisen. It was a privilege to visit the Center and meet the staff - a worthwhile project!

Alcoholism

They promise them freedom,
while they themselves are slaves of depravity
for a man is a slave to whatever has mastered him.
1Peter 2:19

Cheryl often asked me to pray for her. But whenever I asked her why, she would only say, "I'm going through a downer." What she didn't want me or anyone else to know that she was struggling with alcohol. Like most alcoholics, she lived in continuous denial was addicted to something that was tearing her life apart.

Finally, I confronted Cheryl and asked if she were, as I suspected, addicted to alcohol. She couldn't bring herself to use the word "addicted." Instead, she admitted only, "I have a slight problem in the area sometimes."

A controversy rages over whether addiction to alcohol is a "disease" or sin. Let's be clear on one thing. Addiction to anything apart from Jesus Christ in sin. It's true that almost any addiction to anything apart from Jesus Christ is sin. Its true that almost any addiction may make a person sick. But to excuse drunkenness and whitewash it by calling it a "disease" is to minimize it and almost deny the problem exists.

If drunkenness is a sickness," it's the only disease:

- that is contracted by an act of the wall?
- that requires a license for distribution;
- that is bottled and sold;
- that requires outlets for its sale;
- that produces revenue for the government;
- that promotes crime;
- that is habit-forming and promoted by untold millions of dollars in adverting;
- for which we are fined and imprisoned when we exhibit its adverse symptoms;
- which produces thousands of deaths on our highways each month;
- which has no bacterial or viral cause, and for which there is no corrective medicine.

You may be saying, "How do I know whether I'm really addicted to alcohol, or I just like to drink?

Many years ago a man who had been delivered from drunkenness traveled across this country lecturing on the evils of alcohol. He told me ten simple questions to ask to find out if someone is really addicted. If you answer "yes" to one of the questions, you may be an addict; if you answered "yes" to any two , you probably are addicted to alcohol; if you answer "yes" to any. You definitely are an alcohol.

- Do I crave a drink at a specific time each day?
- Do I gulp my drinks and sneak extras?
- Do I drink to relieve feeling of inadequacy?
- Do I drink to escape worry and to dispel the blues?
- Do I drink when overly tired in order to "get a grip"?
- Is drinking affecting my peace of mind?
- Is drinking making my home life unhappy?
- Do I prefer to drink alone?
- Do I require a drink the "next morning" ?
- Do I miss time at work or am I ineffective on the job because of my drinking?

Many excuse their propensity for drunkenness by saying it doesn't hurt anyone but himself or herself. But is this really true?

As I write this, I have just finished reading a news report about anti-nuclear power plant protesters in my state. They take their cause very seriously. But isn't alcoholism a much greater threat to our safety?

What if sixty or seventy people were killed daily by malfunctioning nuclear power plants?
What if such problems seriously injured 1500 people daily?
What if the presence of nuclear power plants caused another 250 people to suffer permanent brain damage daily?
What if existence of those power plants caused fifteen people to commit suicide every day?
What if it caused $35 billion a year in damages?

Our federal government would outlaw nuclear power plants immediately. Yet the above tells the story of damage caused by alcohol only is it not consider outlawed, it is also seen as a good source of a large tax base for local, state. And federal governments.

How low have we slipped? A full decade ago we already knew alcohol was a leading cause of 50 percent of all automobile fatalities, 80 percent of all home violence, 60 percent of all child abuse, and 30 percent of all suicides.

It is envisioned that once this program has been piloted by the Living Word Biblical Counseling Center, it can be replicated in various churches and regions since the program implemented to the center's certification program will be involved in delivering the program to its clients (Counselees). Participants in the pilot program will come from varied sources, referrals from the court system, churches, or other agencies. A long - term benefit of this program is the fact that the process is not only confined to overcoming drug addiction but also applying it to other sins such as alcoholism, lying, stealing, etc. Some participants will be placed in the New Jersey Work Force Program and others in the educational sector.

Solution:

To address the drug addiction problem that appears to be the increase and in particular among Black males the center is proposing implementation of program Twelve Steps Back to God Throughout Jesus Christ. The program is specifically designated to deliver persons from drug addiction through its intense used of four major components.

So, there is no way drinking can be justified by a believer. If you find yourself addicted to alcohol and you've never accepted Jesus Christ as your Savior, that's the first step. No human power can set you free, only the divine power that comes by trusting Jesus Christ as your Savior.

If you are a Christian and you're struggling in this area, there is wonderful hope for you. Jesus Christ already lives within you. His power and love can set you free from the bondage to drink!

Counsel from God's Word

Steps that will set you from alcoholism:

1. **Admit that drunkenness is sin, not just a social problem.**

   God's Word says, "Wine is a mocker, and beer a brawler, whoever is led astray by them is not wise" (Proverbs 20:1) Solomon also observed:

   Who has woe? Who has a sorrow? Who has strife? Who has complaints? Who has needless bruises? Who has bloodshot eyes? Those who linger over wine, who go to sample bowls of mixed wine. Do not gaze at wine when it is red, when it sparkles in the cup, when it goes down smoothly! In the end it bites like a snake and poisons like a viper. Your eyes will see strange sights, and mind imagine confusing things (Proverbs 23:29-33).

   The New Testament certainly isn't silent about the sin of drunkenness. The apostle Paul state clearly: "Do not get drunk on wine, which leads to debauchery" (Ephesians 5:18a)

   Don't rationalize your drinking away and produce excuses about why you can't help you. The quicker you acknowledge that getting drunk is a sin against God and Others, the quicker you can be delivered.

2. **Decide now to never drink alcoholic beverages again try to "taper" off slowly.**

   God wants you to walk away from alcoholism now and decide to never drink again. You may feel you're too weak to make that commitment, but it can be done. Remember, you have almighty God and His Word to back you up!

Don't forget that we "can do everything through him who gives [us] strength" *(Philippians 4:13)*. The Lord promises, never will I leave you and never will I forsake you *"(Hebrews 13:5b)*. No matter how bad your problem is, God invites you to " Call to me and I will answerer you and tell you great and unreachable things you do not know" *(Jeremiah 33:3)*.

God has promised to provide His presence and His power for you to forsake this sin.

3. **Establish new friends and relationships.**

   One reason many cannot stop drinking is that all the friends they keep drink. If that's true for you, seek immediately to establish acquaintances and build friendships with teetotalers, so the temptation to drink when you're with others won't occur. Scripture warns: "Do not be misled. Bad company corrupts good character" *(1 Corinthians 15:33)*

4. **Become accountable to a group of godly people and meet regularly with them.**

   "Iron sharpens iron." It makes a positive difference when we have someone to whom to report weekly, someone who is willing to ask us the hard questions. Elisha had Elijah, Timothy had Paul. You need someone too.

   James tells us to "confess your sins to each other and pray for each other so that you may be healed" *(James 5:16a)*.

5. **Remember that if for some reason you slip and drink again, God's grace is adequate and His forgiveness is available.**

   God won't erase the consequences of our failure and sin, but 1 John 1:9 Tells us God is faithful and just and will forgive our sins. Even in times of Greatest discouragement, the Lord says to us: My grace is sufficient for You, for my power is made perfect in weakness " *(2 Corinthians 12:9)*. That's a great and reassuring promise of God for you.

6. **Remind yourself daily why it's wrong for you to drink.**

Alcoholism is wretched. Never forget that:

- it harms your body:
- it makes you a slave:
- it is poor stewardship of your time, money, and health;
- it may cause another believer to fall into sin;
- it dishonors the Holy Spirit who has made your body His temple *(1 Corinthians 3:16);*
- it supports an industry whose product brings poverty and death.

More biblical counsel:

1 Corinthians 6:9,10
Romans 14:21
Proverbs 23:20
2 Corinthians 5:17
John 8:36
1 Corinthians 10:13
Proverbs 28:13
Isaiah 26:3
Matthew 11:28
Galatians 5:22,23

Projects Activities

Transportation

The final goal of our Twelve Step Back to God Program should be job training leading to a good paying job in a growing industry.

Freight transportation by truck is a billion dollar per year business. I can train personnel essential to trucking such as dispatch and administrative workers, mechanics and maintenance, as well as drivers. The only educational requirement for these jobs is a high school diploma or equivalent and the specialized training that we provide. Each course of training will have a full cirrocumuli including on job training at the freight business, we will start and operate. This business in addition to providing job training and job opportunity can be operated profitably enough to support itself and other ministries and programs operated by the **501- C- 3**. The training program will staff the business, the business will provide equipment and training facilities as well as financial support and jobs for the program participant.

The following are outlines for job training:

Job title: *Dispatcher / Administrative Worker*

A. learn all forms used in Trucking Business
   - *Uniform Bill of Lading*
   - *Log Book*
   - *Dispatch Sheet*
   - *Files paperwork*
   - *Rating & Routing*

B. Mechanic and Truck Maintenance
   - *Simple truck repairs and diagnosis*
   - *Tire repair and replacement*
   - *Routine maintenance of Truck and air break system*
   - *Checking and replacing lubricants*

C. **Truck driver**

   - Safe operation and movement of loaded 18 wheeler, 80,000 lb. Gross weight tractor and trailer
   - Techniques of securing freight to truck for movement

D. Owner / Operator

- All participant completing all three courses of study will be qualified to become an owner / operator. That is an independent truck owner business person who can lease himself and his quuipment to any common carrier he wishes to work with based on criteria important to him such as compensation, where and when you work etc.

- We owner / operator is progressively becoming the backbone off the truck teamsportation industry. The work is steady and hard but the compensation is fair. One major criteria is necessary for all of the above listed positions, you must be drug free. Random testing is a mandatory requirement in each position.

By Gregory Hood

Employment Concept
Developed by a student enrolled in the Course
Biblical Counseling (3).
Rita Freeney

Rita Freeney   Biblical Counseling 3
October 6th 2003
Subject Presentation   Unemployment

1. **Purpose of Work "A display of God's glory."**
    a. Work is a spiritual matter.
    b. The entire universe is set up to work as a unit supporting each other.
    C. Benefits of Work .

        1   Healthy physically.
        2   Healthy emotionally.
        3   Healthy spiritually.

    D. Work - God's view says work is positive.

        1   Work is a partnership with God Gen. 1:28-31
        2. Christ has leadership over work. Ephesians 1:22
        3. Work helps us to provide for the poor. Proverbs 31:17-20
        4. God designed work to provide for us and our families. 1 Thessalonians 2:9

    E. Unemployment is the opposite of God's design.

11. **Unemployment effects the spiritual, mental, and physical part of man.**

        a. Experience lack of self worth.
        b. Defective self-image

        1. Sense of being unsatisfied or unfulfilled
        2. Feeling down
        3. Depression - hopelessness

111.**Unemployment can be deeply effected by root problems.**

   a. Root problem make it difficult to get a job and keep that job.
   b. Root problems need to be addressed and dealt with by replacing sinful disobedient behavior with actions that are in line with God's Word.
   c. Some root problems are:

       1. Selfishness, greed, malice
       2. Pride, envy, deceit, laziness
       3. Self - pity, jealousy.

IV. **Unemployment can be related to the person not aware of his / her natural God - given talents.**

       1. Someone with an aptitude for math may do well in accounting.
       2. Mechanically talented - working in the area of fixing things
       3. Knowing your gift promote satisfaction, reward, a healthy challenge to grow in the area, a desire to be promoted in knowledge, position, or contentment of how their talent helps others, all of which give Glory to God.

V. **Unemployment - The Job Search - Priority - Putting yourself in Gods hands.**

   A. Begins with a proper relationship with God. (3 prerequisites)

       1. Recognizing and accepting the lordship of Christ. Galatians 2:19,20
       2. Having a pure heart; willingness to hear Proverbs 16:1-3
       3. Being sensitive to the Lord's timing. Romans 1:8-15

   B. Once completing 1,2, & 3, this is the time to begin the search.

       1. Get up every morning to search five days a week for eight hours daily.
       2. Develop the attitude to get an honest job as long as I can do the work and not do anything to harm the cause of Christ.
       3. Don't quit a job until you have another job.
       4. Leave a job in a manner that you would be able to go back and be re-employed if you had to.
       5. Don't have an attitude that the job offered is beneath you.

C. If you find that you are still not able to meet your obligations there are two possibilities:

      a. Decrease your spending
      b. Get additional training for a job that will pay for what you need.

VI. The Resume

a. A summary of your previous work experience, education and accomplishments.
b. A personal sales brochure
c. To convince someone to interview for the job opening.

      1. Help the counsel know this is hard work. (Homework Assignment)
      2. Keep them committed until the resume is done.
      3. One page, well designed, airy looking, high quality.

d. Motivational questions that will help in preparing the resume or for the interview.

      1. What are my skills?
      2. What are my strengths?
      3. What are my Qualifications?
      4. What are my accomplishments?
      5. What do I know about my perceptive employer and what does he / she expect my qualifications to be>
      6. What are the items employer's included in the criteria?

VII. The job Interview
    A. An opportunity for you to meet the employer.
    1. Be neat and be on time.
    2. Be aware of verbal and nonverbal communication (body language)
    3. Have a copy of your resume.
    B. Lying during the interview is not acceptable and violates the laws of God.

VIII. Profile of a typical unemployed man.

A. Laziness
B. Immaturity
C. Dependency
D. Irresponsibility
E. Hopelessness
F. Addiction
G. Lack of Education
H. Blaming others.

IX. Other Information to share.

- Change of the way men are taught from generation to generation.
- Codependency can delay the ability of the unemployed person to see the root issues.
- The unemployed person is often a product of bad parenting—failure to properly train children to be responsible, self sufficient and obedient to God's word.
- Additional comments from a person whose difference in age may see things differently from the author of the book and the tape.

Things have changed drastically since the writing of this book. The job market has changed limiting the number of jobs available. Today, many companies are down sizing and replacing personnel with technology to do the man use to do.

Six questions regarding this presentation on unemployment are listed below:

1. Why is unemployment considered sin?
2. What areas of one's life are benefited by employment?
3. What are five of the root problems seen in the life of an unemployed person?
4. What three things need to done before looking for a job?
5. How can poor upbringing affect the mind of a person who experiences habitual unemployment?
6. What three profiles can you find in the life of an unemployed person?
7.

Resource Information:

The Word of God - King James Version
Counseling in African American Communities - Lee N. June
Counseling in African American Communities - lecture by Dr. Willie Richardson

POST - TRAMATIC STRESS DEBRIEFING for COUNSELORS

Observation by the Director:

The Twelve Step Back to God Through Jesus Christ has a group session on Tuesday nights at seven o-clock p.m. The director observe two of the group participates appear to be glasses eye, noise running and the shakes. One of the participate was question about his appearance. His response was that he had been to the Doctors because of his Allegeages and the medices the Doctor gave him. The other participate did not say anything. We continues to work with another client. The male who was question when to rest room; his return he whisper in the director ear, you thorght you had me. The next day the participate **OD's**. There was a major concerns from those counselor who work with him one on one. There was know debriefing for counselor or the group. There was some talk in group. Three to Six months the other participate who was getting **High** the one who **OD's** confess that it has been on his mind, that they where getting high for the last time.

The Living Word Biblical Counseling Program, **Twelve Steps Back To God Through Jesus Christ,** has put in place the following process: develop by Joanne Graham. There has been other situation that counselor has been involve in and the case did not work the way it was design.

Joanne Graham
Instructor: Mr. Richard Lee
BC-3
December 12, 2005

POST-TRAMATIC STRESS DEBRIEFING FOR COUNSELORS

Debriefing has been widely advocated for routine use following major traumatic events. While several methods of debriefing have been described, the information which I have reviewed indicates that most researchers consider debriefing as a "single-session semi-structured crisis intervention designed to reduce and prevent unwanted psychological sequelae following traumatic events, by promoting emotional processing through the ventilation and normalization of reactions and preparation for possible future experiences"

Debriefing was first described as a group intervention and considered to be part of a comprehensive, systematic, multi-component approach to the management of traumatic stress, but it has also been used with individuals and as a stand-alone intervention. Its purpose is to review the impressions and reactions of clients shortly after a traumatic incident. The focus is on the present reactions of those involved.

DEBRIEFING CHRISTIAN COUNSLORS AFTER A CATASTROPHIC EVENT

This level of debriefing must be based on a multi-strand approach.   Clearly, time is of the essence when confronted with a major disaster such as that experienced during Hurricane Katrina.   There is little time to prepare for what may lie ahead.   Therefore, for the purposes of this report, I will assume that the individuals being called upon to assist in a major disaster, such as the above-mentioned crisis, are responding to a situation of this proportion for the first time.   Although these are well trained Christian Counselors, they have no prior experience in dealing with such a catastrophe.   Thus an effective debriefing tool should consist of the following:

1. If time permits, an effective debriefing model should cover expectations and realities tailored to the specific situation to be confronted. This session should begin and end with prayer.

2. Since the crisis could last for several days, some one equipped to monitor and assess impact on counselors should have a critical eye toward observing any untoward or adverse behavioral changes. If any are observed, debriefing of such individuals should take place immediately. This should consist of prayer and finding out what that person is feeling and experiencing at that moment. Prayer must be conducted to help counselor cope with their feelings and to give hope. Counselor must know that God, through His will, has allowed whatever is happening to take place. We are not to judge, only to help.

3. Immediately after the crises, a team debriefing session, consisting of all counselors, whether they exhibit distress on not, should be conducted.

4. Time must be allowed for free expression of feelings

5. This session should begin and end with prayer and thanksgiving regardless of the outcome of the disaster.

6. In order to reduce any initial stress, any levels of distress over time and to insure the restoration of function and quality of life with minimal adverse effects, counselors should be encouraged to talk freely about their experience, how it impacted them and their faith, and how they feel about it. Again, as with all sessions, this one should begin and end with prayer and thanksgiving and the building of hope.

7. Since acute stress disorder occurs within a month after a traumatic event, a minimum of 3 follow-up sessions should follow, each no more than one week apart, to ensure that counselors are returning to pre-traumatic normalcy.

8. In cases were counselors are experiencing higher and increased levels of distress, they should be provided individual counseling to augment the group sessions. It is important that they attend both so that they can no that they are not alone. What they are experiencing is a normal part of the process of having undergone a very traumatic experience.

9. In all cases following a traumatic event, counselors should be given a 24 hour contact who will talk and pray with them as need.

10. Individuals who may not express the need for such service, should be contacted at least once per week between sessions or as the Holy Spirits leads to insure that they are alright. Prayer should be offered each time.

To sum it up, debriefing is a process of helping people reflect on their experience. It can be conducted in a group setting or individually; during the experience or after it has occurred. There is no one right way to debrief. However, those providing the debriefing must be well trained in order to assess:

- To what degree debriefing is required;

- If the level of debriefing being offered is adequate;

- If more intensive intervention is required;

- The level and type of appropriate follow-up necessary.

And most importantly, as Christians, we have our faith in God to help us help other believers through such challenging circumstances. We must allow our understanding and belief to guide us in this process of spiritual restoration.

**Our Father which art in heaven, Hollowed be thy name.
Thy kingdom come.
Thy will be done in earth, as it is in heaven.
Give us this day our daily bread.
And forgive us our debts, as we forgive our debtors.
And lead us not into temptation, but deliver us from evil:
For thine is the kingdom, and the power,
and the glory, for ever. Amen.**

As Jesus instructed the disciples about what He wanted them to do, He said in effect, "This is how you should pray," not, "This is what you should pray." He then proceeded with a model prayer in which He addressed several areas of concern that we can rightly take to God. He first revealed how to address His Father and showed the importance of focusing attention on the furtherance of God's kingdom. It was only after this that He spoke of expressing to God one's personal needs and requests.

The one to whom we pray should be uppermost in our thoughts. Jesus taught that believers can address God in a way that reveals both His personal relationship with us and His transcendence (preeminence and supremacy). He is "Our Father." This means those who have received His Son as personal Saviour have an intimate, familial relationship with Him.

Three requests relative to who He is follow. First is "hollowed be thy name" that is, He is to be set apart as holy and respected. It is a request that He help us speak and live lives that reflect properly upon Him. The second request is "Thy kingdom come." This is a request that God help us to be faithful and obedient in living out the kingdom principles and thus be effective in spreading the good news about Jesus Christ. The third request is "Thy will be done in earth, as it is in heaven." We need to recognize our need for His help in doing His will consistently.

It is easy to neglect talking to God about Himself and His will when we pray. Too often we move quickly to our own needs and concerns instead of taking time to speak with God about His concerns and interests.

There is no need to read a special meaning into the request for daily bread. It is simply a realization that we are totally dependent on God for every provision. In Jesus' day there were many living at or near poverty levels. They literally did not know from one day to the next whether they were going to eat.

God is our Provider for every physical need, but this should also remind us that He does not always provide far in advance. It is too bad that so many are so wealthy that they miss the joy of seeing God provide day by day. Special needs do arise, however, that remind us of our dependence on God for physical needs. Health concerns can be such a reminder. However much we might have of this world's goods, we should never take them for granted but rather accept and enjoy them with deep gratitude to the Provider.

It is clear that Jesus was referring to sins when He spoke of "debts." Our sins put us in debt to God, and we must be forgiven if those request seems to be the heart of the concluded the prayer. There is also a condition attached. We are to seek forgiveness in the same way we forgive others does not buy our forgiveness, but it does reveal that we belong to God, who has forgiven us.

Giving in to temptation is what gets us into trouble. It brings guilt upon us and thus the need for forgiveness. Once we have been for forgiven, we can avoid further guilt by not responding to further temptation. Even in this, however, we are in desperate need of God's help. This final request recognizes the power of sin and our ability to overcome it successfully on our own. "Evil" here can be translated "the evil one." If that is how we should understand it, it reinforces the power that stands behind the temptation to sin.

"Let no man say when he is tempted, I am tempted with evil, neither tempted he any man: but every man is tempted, when he is drawn away of his own lust, and enticed." There is a real person behind such temptations. We know him as Satin. He is far too powerful for us to handle on our own. We need God's assistance if we are to stan against the temptations that come our way through Satin and his hosts.

We are part of God's kingdom, to whom belong power and glory forever. This doxological ending appears to have come from 1ˢᵗ Chronicles 29:11.

Jesus again spoke of the need for forgiving others. Ephesians 4:32 reminds us that we are to "be ...kind one another, tenderhearted, forgiving one another, even as God for Christ's sake hath forgiven you. "It is difficult to explain how a Christian can carry grudges against others. We are God's children only because we have repented of our sins and been forgiven. After having been forgiven so much, how dare we refuse to forgive those who wrong us? If we want to enjoy our own forgiveness to the fullest, we will forgive others.

SERENITY PRAYER

God, grant me the serenity

To accept the things I cannot change,

The courage to change the things I can,

and the wisdom to know the difference,

Living one day at a time,

Enjoying one moment at a time,

Accepting hardship as a pathway to a time,

Taking, as Jesus did,

This sinful world as it is,

Not as I would have it;

Trusting that you will make all things right if I surrender your will,

So that I may be reasonably happy in this life

And supremely happy with you forever in the next.

Amen

Biblical Scriptures Needed for Recovery

Action {Walk what you talk}

* Corinthians 4:20
* Galatians 5:16-26
* Ephesians 4:1-3
* Ephesians 5:15-18
* Ephesians 5:1,2
* Isaiah 30:21
* Romans 6:1-4

Bitterness

* Exodus 16:1-3
* Proverbs 10:12
* James 5:9
* Ephesians 4:4:31,32
* 1 John 2:9-11
* Matthew 7:1-5
* Hebrews 12:14,15

Courage

* Psalm 143:5-10
* Philippians 1:27,28
* John 16:33
* Psalm 91
* Psalm 28:6-9
* Psalm 118:5-7
* Psalm 34:1,2
* Psalm 27:14
* Psalm 46:1,2
* Ephesians 6:10-17

Discouragement

* Hebrews 12:12-15
* Hebrews 12:3,4
* Revelation 21:3,4
* Psalm 4:1-7
* Psalm 42:1-7
* 2 Corinthians 4:15-18
* Psalm 61:1-5
* Psalm 73:26

Anger / Resentment

* James 1:19,20
* Proverbs 19:11, 20:22
* Leviticus 19:18
* Psalm 37:8-11
* Proverbs 15:1
* Matthew 5:5-21
* Peter 3:8-18

Blame

* Genesis 3:9-15
* Luke 14:15-24
* Exodus 32:19-24
* Romans 1:20
* 1 Samuel 13:11-14
* Jeremiah 1:6,7
* 1 Samuel 15:16-32

Dependence Upon God

* 2 Chronicles 20:6-12
* John 15:5
* Psalm 127: 1
* 2 Corinthians 3:4,5
* Jeremiah 10:23,24
* Psalm 139:1-5
* Deuteronomy 33:27
* Proverbs 3:5-6

Easy Does It

* Ecclesiastes 7:8,9
* Titus 2:2
* Romans 12:12
* Hebrews 10:36
* James 1:2-4
* James 5:7
* Psalm 94:19

Faith

* Matthew 6:30
* Mark 9:14-24
* Matthew 8:23-27
* Romans 5:1,2
* Mark 11:24,25
* 1 Peter 5:7
* James 1:5-8
* Romans 4:18-25
* Peter 1:7-9
* Ephesians 6:13-17

Fear

* Psalm 118:5,6
* Psalm 34:4
* Romans 8:38,39
* Psalm 46:1-10
* Jeremiah 1:6-9
* Psalm 112:1-8
* Psalm 143:1-10
* Psalm 27:1-3
* Isaiah 43:1,2
* Psalm 32:7
* Psalm 118:5-9
* 1 John 4:18

Freedom

* John 8:32
* Romans 6:1,2
* Romans 7:21-25
* Galatians 5:1
* 1 Peter 1:2
* Psalm 107:16
* Colossians 1:12-14
* Acts 13:29-38
*

Forgiveness

* Genesis 50:14-21
* Psalm 65:3
* Psalm 103. 1-12
* Acts 13:38,39
* John 1:16,17
* Matthew 6:14,15
* Philippians 3:13,14
* Mark 11:24,25
* Isaiah 43:2-26
* Luke 17:1-4
* Ephesians 1:6-9
* Psalm 32:1-5

Friendship With God

* Psalm 147:1-11
* James 4:4-10
* Proverbs 18:24
* Psalm 25:14
* John 15:13,14
* Job 16:20-22
* Exodus 33:1
* Hebrews 13:5,6

Gratitude

* Colossians 1:12-14
* Psalm 106:1,2
* Luke 17:11-19
* Psalm 9:11-12
* 1 Peter 2:9,10
* Luke 15:11-32
* Colossians 3:15

Humility

* Proverbs 22:4
* 1 Corinthians 1:3-16
* Mark 9:35
* Psalm 69:32,33
* Micah 6:8
* James 3:13-18
* Romans 12:1-3
* James 4:5-10
* Proverbs 29:23

Guilt

* Genesis 3:8-10
* Psalm 51:11-15
* Romans 5:20-21
* Romans 7:15-17
* Isaiah 53:6
* Romans 3:23,24
* James 2:10
* Romans 5:8,9
* Galatians 3:21,22

Healing

* Mark 5:21-34
* Psalm 27:4-6
* Isaiah 61:1
* James 5:16
* Psalm 147:3-5
* Hebrews 2:14,15
* 1 Corinthians 6:9-12
* Isaiah 53:3-5
* Luke 13:10-13
* Hosea 5:15- 6:3
* Mark 2:17
* Psalm 107:10-22

Joy

* Psalm 69:29-33
* Proverbs 13:12
* Psalm 28: 6,7
* Psalm 33:20-22
* Isaiah 12
* Psalm 34:1-3
* Psalm 42:4-8
* Psalm 32:1

Let Go & Let God

* 2 Corinthians 1:9
* Psalm 46:1,2
* Psalm 33:18-22
* Psalm 42:9-11
* Psalm 39:1-7
* Jeremiah 17L7,8
* James 4:10

Loneliness

* Psalm 68:6
* Ecclesiastes 4:9,10
* Psalm 146:
* 1 Peter 3:8
* 1 John 1:7
* Psalm 31:20-22
* Matthew 28:18-20

Live & Let Live

* Luke 10:38-42
* 1 Thessalonians 4:11
* Matthew 7:1-5
* Romans 2:1
* 1 Corinthians 4:5
* James 5:9
* 1 Corinthians 2:11

Love

* 1 John 4:7-10
* Romans 8:35-39
* Galatians 2:20
* Colossians 3:12-15
* Deuteronomy 10:12
* 1 Peter 4:7-10
* John 3:16
* John 15:9-14
* John 13:34,35

Newness of Life

* Romans 6:1-4
* Colossians 3:9-14
* Luke 15:11-24
* Romans 12:1,2
* Romans 8:11-14
* Ephesians 2:1-10
* 2 Peter 1:2-9
* Psalm 51:7-15
* Ezekiel 11:19,20
* Philippians 4:8,9
* 2 Corinthians 5:17
* 1 Timothy 4:7-10

Obedience

* 1 John 5:1-5
* Mathew 7:24-29
* 1 John 2:12-14 ,17
* James 2:12,13
* 1 Samuel 12:22,23
* Acts 5:28,29
* John 15:9,10
* 1 Chronicles

One Day at a Time

* Luke 12:25,26
* Luke 12:11,12
* Philippians 4:6
* 1 Peter 5:7
* Matthew 6:25-34
* James 4:13-16
* Psalm 110:3
* Proverbs 27:1
* Philippians 3:13,14

Overcoming

* John 16:33
* Romans 12:21
* Romans 13:11-14
* John 8:30-32
* 2 timothy 3:14-17
* Nahum 1:7
* Psalm 40:1,2
* Isaiah 40:28-31
* 1 John 5:1-5

Patience

* James 1:2-4
* Psalm 37:7
* Ecclesiastes 7:8
* Psalm 27:14
* Romans 12:12
* Hebrews 10:36
* James 5:7-11
* Psalm 116:1,2

Open – Mindedness

* Matthew 16:23
* John 9:39
* Hebrews 3:10
* Ephesians 3:20,21
* Isaiah 30:21
* Isaiah 55:8,9
* Mark 9:23
* Proverbs 18:15
* Matthew 21:28-32

Pain

* Psalm 50:14,15
* 1 Peter 5:8-11
* Romans 8:17,18
* Hebrews 11:24,25
* Isaiah 53:5,6
* 2 Corinthians 4:7-18
* 1 Peter 4:1-5
* James 5:10,11
* Mark 14:32 38
* Hebrews 2:9,10

Relapse / Slips

* Psalm 26:12
* 1 Corinthians 10:12,13
* 1 Peter 1:14-14
* 1 Peter 2:9
* Romans 6:1-4
* James 1:13-15
* Psalm 71:20,21
* Romans 7:15-25
* Psalm 119:105
* Psalm 55:22
* James 4:6-10
* Philippians 4:6,7
* Psalm 94:17,18

Recovery / Sobriety

* Ephesians 5:1,2
* Ephesians 4:1-7
* Deuteronomy 29:6
* Isaiah 43:112
* Mark 8:34-38
* 1 Peter 2:10
* Romans 8:30-32
* 1 Peter 2:10
* Hebrews 12:12-15
* Philippians 3:13,14
* Ephesians 4:17-32
* Psalm 116:1-9
* Ephesians 5:6-11
* Romans 13:12-14
* Galatians 5:16-26
* Philippians 1:6

Serenity / Peace

* Matthew 5:6-10
* Isaiah 26:3
* Psalm 5:11
* Colossians 3:15
* Jeremiah 15:16
* John 15:9-12
* 1 Peter 1:8,9
* Psalm 146:3-9
* Philippians 4:4-7

Temptation

* Hebrews 4:12-16
* Matthew 26:41
* James 1:2-8
* 1 Corinthians 10:13
* Hebrews 2:14-18
* 2 Thessalonians 3:1-5
* James 4:12-18
* Proverbs 4:14-19
* Ephesians 6:12-14
* Romans 6:12-14
* 1 Peter 5:8,9

Religion

* Deuteronomy 10:12,13
* James 1:26,27
* Ecclesiastes 12:13
* Hosea 6:6
* Romans 13:8-10
* Mark 12:28-34

Stumbling Blocks

* Ephesians 5:3-9
* 1 Corinthians 10:3-12
* 1 John 5:18-21
* 1 Corinthians 8:9
* 1 Peter 2:7,8
* Ephesians 5:1-9

Vengeance

* Proverbs 20:22
* Leviticus 19:18
* Proverbs 24:28,29
* Matthew 5:38,39
* Romans 12: 14-21
* 1 Peter 3:9

Will of God

*   Psalm 40:6-8
*   Ephesians 6:6,7
*   Psalm 143:5-11
*   James 4:13-17
*   Matthew 26:41,42
*   Romans 8:28
*   Proverbs 16:1
*   John 6:25-29
*   Romans 12:1,2

Wisdom

*   Proverbs 2:1-9
*   Job 28:28
*   Psalm 111:10
*   James 3:17,18
*   Proverbs 4:7-9
*   Hosea 14:9
*   Colossians 3:16,17
*   Matthew 7:24-29
*   Ecclesiastes 7:11,12
*   2 Timothy 3:14-17

Willingness

*   Isaiah 1:18,19
*   Psalm 51:10-12
*   1 Chronicles 28:9
*   Philippians 2:13
*   2 Corinthians 8;10,11
*   Romans 12:1,2

In Loving Memory
of
Gregory L. Hood

Sunrise
January 7, 1947

Sunset
October 27, 2008